Living Abundantly

Volume 3

by Theodore H. Epp

Director
Back to the Bible Broadcast

75¢

Back to the Bible Broadcast

Box 82808   Lincoln, Nebraska 68501

85,000 printed to date—1973
(5-2514—85M—93)

Printed in the United States of America

Contents

Contents

Chapter 1

The Believer's Spiritual Conflict
(Eph. 6:10-20)

There are three lines of truth unfolded in the Book of
Ephesians. Each is an outgrowth of the other. First, there is
the teaching of the believer's exalted position in Jesus Christ,
as set forth in the first three chapters of Ephesians. Everyone
who has received Christ as Saviour has this perfect position.
The teaching concerning this position reveals what Christ has
done for the believer.

Second, the Book of Ephesians concerns the believer's
spiritual walk on this earth, based on his exalted position in
Christ. This subject is emphasized in the last three chapters of
Ephesians through verse 9 of chapter 6. This passage tells of
what Christ wants to accomplish in the believer's "walk," or
life.

Third, the Book of Ephesians concludes with teaching
about the believer's spiritual conflict. Here Christ is seen
working *through* the believer.

Some ask, Why the conflict? Why end the epistle on a
battlefield?

Perhaps it seems strange that after the book reveals the
lofty position each believer has in Christ and the noble walk
that every believer is to have, it then dwells on warfare.
Throughout Ephesians we have noted that Christ has won the
victory for the believer. Chapter 4 tells us that "he led
captivity captive" (v. 8); that is, He led captive those who
held us captive. So if we are victorious in Him, why the
conflict?

It is a characteristic of believers to want to remain "on
the mountaintop." This was true of Peter when he, along
with James and John, witnessed the Transfiguration of the

5

Lord on the mountaintop. They not only saw Christ in all of His glory, but they also saw Moses and Elijah talking with Him. It was such a thrilling experience that Peter said to the Lord, "It is good for us to be here: if thou wilt, let us make here three tabernacles; one for thee, and one for Moses, and one for Elias [Elijah] " (Matt. 17:4). But this was not to be done; they had to return to the valley. One cannot stay on the mountaintop; he must return to the duties of life to serve Jesus Christ in these activities also.

Reasons for Spiritual Conflict

There are three reasons why a believer can expect—and must be prepared for—a spiritual conflict as he lives for the Lord. First, believers must be prepared for spiritual warfare because there is a traitor in the camp. This traitor is the "flesh," which is the old nature. The old nature is not eradicated when a person receives Christ as Saviour, so there is a spiritual struggle between the old nature and the new nature in the life of each believer.

Galatians 5:17 says, "For the flesh lusteth against the Spirit, and the Spirit against the flesh: and these are contrary the one to the other: so that ye cannot do the things that ye would." Here we see the flesh opposing the liberty we have in Christ. The flesh always seeks to bring us into bondage to its desires. Satan entices us through the flesh. Jesus had to rebuke Peter one time and say, "Simon, Simon, behold, Satan hath desired to have you, that he may sift you as wheat: but I have prayed for thee, that thy faith fail not" (Luke 22:31,32).

Satan is the enemy of our souls; he is envious of our salvation in Christ and especially seeks to destroy our allegiance to Christ. Satan trails believers and tries to take advantage of them. The Bible tells us, "Be sober, be vigilant; because your adversary the devil, as a roaring lion, walketh about, seeking whom he may devour: whom resist stedfast in the faith" (I Pet. 5:8,9).

A second reason there is spiritual conflict is that the believer is a member of the Body of Christ. From the time that God pronounced the curse on Satan in the Garden of Eden, Satan has sought to destroy Christ. Therefore, anyone associated with Christ—especially a part of His Body—is subject to Satan's attack. There are many instances recorded throughout the Scriptures when Satan sought to destroy Christ. When Christ took upon Himself a body to be born among men to die for their sin, Satan sought to destroy Him as a baby. Herod served Satan's purpose when he decreed that all the children in Bethlehem and surrounding areas, two years old and under, should be killed (Matt. 2:16). However, because God is wiser than Satan, Jesus escaped death because Mary and Joseph had been instructed to take Him out of the country.

Later, when Satan tried to entice Jesus to sin, he challenged Christ to throw Himself down from a pinnacle of the temple, but Christ responded, "Thou shalt not tempt the Lord thy God" (4:7). When Jesus was on the cross, Satan no doubt thought he was victorious in having Christ put to death, but Christ rose from the dead and thereby proved that He had conquered Satan. Christ then ascended to the Father, beyond the realm of Satan.

Inasmuch as Satan can no longer attack Christ Himself, Satan attacks the Body of Christ which is the Church. The mystical Body of Christ, made up of all believers, is within the reach of Satan even though Christ Himself is not. However, the Body of Christ will ultimately be victorious, for Christ said, "I will build my church; and the gates of hell shall not prevail against it" (16:18).

A third reason there is spiritual conflict for believers is that God's plan and purpose include the fact that Christ will someday rule the world in righteousness. Because this refers to a future time, this might be referred to as a "dispensational" reason for spiritual conflict. As the Apostle John told of a vision he had had of Christ's return to earth, he said, "And I saw heaven opened, and behold a white horse; and he that sat upon him was called Faithful and True, and in righteousness he doth judge and make war" (Rev. 19:11). Acts 17:31 prophesies, "Because he [God] hath appointed a day, in the which he will judge the world in righteousness by that man whom he hath ordained; whereof he hath given assurance unto all men, in that he hath raised him from the dead." This verse reveals that the Father has delegated all judgment to the Son. This means—and Satan knows this—that there will be a final reckoning with the powers of evil, which will result in their—and Satan's—ultimate destruction. In Revelation 1:18 Christ says, "I am he that liveth, and was dead; and, behold, I am alive for evermore, Amen; and have the keys of hell and of death." Revelation 20:10 tells of the final doom of Satan: "And the devil that deceived them was cast into the lake of fire and brimstone, where the beast and the false prophet are, and shall be tormented day and night for ever and ever."

Inasmuch as believers are to share with Christ in His reigning and judging, we are laid open to the attacks of Satan at the present time. Satan and his messengers claim this world as their own; thus, those of us who will eventually sit in judgment over them are laid open to conflict. Satan is well aware that God's program is closing in on him and for this reason he directs much of his attention to harassing the Church. Even though Satan is at work, the Holy Spirit is at present restraining evil. Second Thessalonians 2:7 says, "For the mystery of lawlessness is already at work; only he who now restrains will do so until he is taken out of the way" (NASB). This restraining work of the Holy Spirit, through believers, has been going on ever since the Day of Pentecost when the Church came into existence. But it is evident we are being brought ever nearer to the final conflict.

Therefore, as Paul wrote his letter to the Ephesians, his final remarks concerning the believer's warfare were necessary and right on target. Believers ought not to be controlled by fear because of this warfare. Rather, we should remember the words of Matthew 16:18: "I will build my church; and the gates of hell shall not prevail against it"; of John 16:33: "In the world ye shall have tribulation: but be of good cheer; I have overcome the world"; and of I John 4:4: "Greater is he that is in you, than he that is in the world."

The Christian does not need to live in constant fear of Satan and his emissaries. Romans 8:31 assures us, "If God be for us, who can be against us?" Paul was writing to believers and the word "if" has the meaning of "since." That is, those of us who have received Jesus Christ as Saviour know that God is for us because Paul has told us this in the preceding passages. Therefore, since God is for us no one is able to stand against us. Paul further explained, "He that spared not his own Son, but delivered him up for us all, how shall he not with him also freely give us all things?" (v. 32). This is where we stand! This is our position in Christ. Thus Paul said, "Who shall lay anything to the charge of God's elect? It is God that justifieth. Who is he that condemneth? It is Christ that died, yea rather, that is risen again, who is even at the right hand of God, who also maketh intercession for us" (vv. 33,34).

The Devil cannot effectively charge us with something now because, having believed in Jesus Christ as Saviour, we have been justified—declared righteous. Though the Devil may bring accusations, Jesus Christ is at the right hand of the Father interceding for us. The Lord Jesus Christ has paid the full penalty for our sin so the Devil—or anyone else—is not able to bring condemnation on us.

Provision for Victory

With these truths in mind concerning our position in Christ, let us now focus our attention on Ephesians 6:10-20. This passage refers to the spiritual warfare in which every believer is involved. It reveals the source of the strength and the equipment we have that enable us to be victorious. We must understand clearly the principles by which this warfare is to be waged. There are certain conditions that must be met if we are to personally experience the victory that Christ has already accomplished for us. It is important to recognize that victory is assumed. Christ has defeated Satan and has won the victory for us. Therefore, our responsibility is to live according to our victorious position and not to suffer defeat at the hands of the Enemy, who has already been defeated. We are to take our stand against any onslaught of the Enemy because he has no chance to defeat us as long as we recognize our position in Christ.

Victory for the believer is the valid promise on which everything else is based. This is seen from Romans 8:35-39. In this passage Paul asked the question, "Who shall separate us from the love of Christ?" (v. 35). After mentioning some things that could be considered possibilities, Paul gave this resounding answer: "Nay, in all these things we are more than conquerors through him that loved us" (v. 37). How can we be more than conquerors? This will be revealed as we examine Ephesians 6:10-20. How wonderful it is to know that nothing "shall be able to separate us from the love of God, which is in Christ Jesus our Lord" (Rom. 8:39).

Paul also reminded the Corinthians of the victory we have in Christ: "But thanks be to God, which giveth us the victory through our Lord Jesus Christ" (I Cor. 15:57). "Now thanks be unto God, which always causeth us to triumph in Christ" (II Cor. 2:14). Ephesians 6:10-20 reveals God's all-sufficient provision for such total victory.

Chapter 2

The Believer's Strength for the Conflict
(Eph. 6:10)

Having told us of our position in Christ and the necessity to put this into practice, Paul said, "Finally, my brethren, be strong in the Lord, and in the power of his might" (Eph. 6:10). From this verse we see that all the power of heaven is at our disposal. This power is available because of our position in Christ that Paul described in the first three chapters of Ephesians. It is only from our position in Christ that the battle can be successfully waged. It's a position of faith—taking God at His Word and trusting Him to do what He said He will do.

This same principle is seen throughout the Scriptures. When the Israelites entered the land of Canaan, God told Joshua, "There shall not any man be able to stand before thee all the days of thy life: as I was with Moses, so I will be with thee: I will not fail thee, nor forsake thee. Be strong and of a good courage: for unto this people shalt thou divide for an inheritance the land, which I sware unto their fathers to give them" (Josh. 1:5,6). Notice that the God of Moses was the God of Joshua, and He is our God also. Again God told Joshua, "Be strong and of a good courage; be not afraid, neither be thou dismayed: for the Lord thy God is with thee whithersoever thou goest" (v. 9).

The word "finally" in Ephesians 6:10 indicates Paul's final word concerning the believer's walk. Paul said, "Be strong in the Lord." Notice he did not say that we are to take our strength *from* the Lord but that we are to be strong *in* the Lord. We are to recognize our position in Christ and live accordingly. As we do this, we will be continuously empowered by the Lord for any conflict. It is important to see that we do not just take our place at the side of the Lord but that our place of strength is in the Lord. Having received Him as Saviour, we are in Him and He is our strength. The word "in" is the key word in the Book of Ephesians. The book reveals how each member of the Body of Christ has its strength in Christ. This is why Paul could say in Philippians 4:13, "I can do all things through Christ which strengtheneth me."

Christ Is Lord

Notice the title "Lord" in Ephesians 6:10. The more common title used throughout Ephesians in referring to the second Person of the Trinity is "Christ." His full title is "Lord Jesus Christ." Each of these three words has a special emphasis. "Jesus" is His earthly name for it was given to Him at birth and has to do with His work of redemption. The angel of the Lord told Joseph, "She [Mary] shall bring forth a son, and thou shalt call his name Jesus: for he shall save his people from their sins" (Matt. 1:21). The name "Christ" is His heavenly name. This is the name Andrew used when he told his brother, " 'We have found the Messiah,' which translated means Christ" (John 1:41, NASB). It has to do with His heavenly work and also His return as the Messiah. In emphasizing our position because of salvation, the Bible most frequently uses the heavenly name, "Christ." This is seen in Galatians 2:20: "I am crucified with Christ: nevertheless I live; yet not I, but Christ liveth in me: and the life which I now live in the flesh I live by the faith of the Son of God, who loved me, and gave himself for me."

The title "Lord" not only reveals His position within the Trinity—He is God—but designates that He is our Master. Remember what Jesus told His disciples: "You call me Teacher, and Lord; and you are right; for so I am" (John 13:13, NASB). Because Jesus Christ is God, He is to be the Master, or Lord, of our lives.

The title "Lord" also reveals the power of Jesus Christ. Referring to the time He will return to earth to destroy His enemies and to establish His kingdom, the Bible says, "And he hath on his vesture and on his thigh a name written, King of Kings, and Lord of Lords" (Rev. 19:16). This is what Jesus is to the believer. He has not only atoned for our sins, but He has overcome our foes by His mighty power. Through death, He has broken Satan's power so that we need not be defeated by him.

This we see in Hebrews 2:14,15: "Since then the children share in flesh and blood, He Himself likewise also partook of the same, that through death He might render powerless him who had the power of death, that is, the devil; and might deliver those who through fear of death were subject to slavery all their lives" (NASB). The same truth is emphasized in Colossians 2:14,15: "Blotting out the handwriting of ordinances that was against us, which was contrary to us, and took it out of the way, nailing it to his cross; and having spoiled principalities and powers, he made a shew of them openly, triumphing over them in it." (Also compare Ephesians 1:19-23 with 4:8).

Christ's resurrection put Him in a position of authority, far above all principalities and powers (Phil. 2:9-11). Because He has all power we are to be "strong in the Lord" (Eph. 6:10), for He is the victorious One. As we think of Him, we must see Him as the Conqueror He is and ourselves as having been raised to the place of conqueror in Him. In Ephesians 2:5,6, Paul wrote that God "even when we were dead in sins, hath quickened us together with Christ, (by grace ye are saved;) and hath raised us up together, and made us sit together in heavenly places in Christ Jesus."

As we have seen, the events in the Book of Joshua illustrate beautifully many of the truths of the Ephesians. Just as Joshua had to recognize the Captain of the Lord's host, so we believers must recognize Christ as the Lord of our lives. Joshua had entered the land of Canaan and before him was the territory that was to be conquered. It seemed almost impossible that the Israelites would be able to take the land as God had promised. But then there appeared a man before him with a drawn sword and Joshua said to him, "Art thou for us, or for our adversaries?" (5:13). The man answered, "Nay; but as captain of the host of the Lord am I now come" (v. 14). Joshua immediately prostrated himself before the man, recognizing him as an appearance of the Lord, and asked, "What saith my lord unto his servant?" The Lord then gave Joshua orders. So we too must recognize Christ as our

Lord and expect Him to guide us and be our strength in battle.

The Book of Joshua presents Jesus Christ as Lord. As the Israelites stood on the border of the Promised Land, the Lord appeared to them as the Conqueror. Joshua had to learn that he could do all things through the Lord, who strengthens believers. The Lord had told Joshua, "Every place that the sole of your foot shall tread upon, that have I given unto you, as I said unto Moses" (1:3). But when the Lord appeared to Joshua, as recorded in chapter 5, He was saying in effect, "I've promised you this land but you must follow Me if you are to take it, for only then will I enable you to take it."

We must remember that the Promised Land is not symbolic of heaven but of abundant life. It was a place filled with conflict, but victory was had as the people took God at His word and lived in obedience to Him. The battles fought in Canaan were won supernaturally. This is evident from events such as the conquering of Jericho. The Israelites marched around Jericho once each day for six days, and on the seventh day they marched around the city seven times. "And it came to pass at the seventh time, when the priests blew with the trumpets, Joshua said unto the people, Shout; for the Lord hath given you the city" (6:16).

Identification With Victory

Many other instances revealed the supernatural working of God in behalf of His people. We must remember that the God of Joshua's time is our God too, that His power has not diminished, and that is available to us through faith. We must not only view Christ as our Captain, having seen Him as the Conqueror, but we must also identify ourselves with Him in His victory. The key to victory is that we must take our position with Christ as a co-victor. We will experience victory on a daily basis as we have faith in Him. Remember, that the evidence of faith is action based on that faith. A faith that does not produce action is not a genuine faith. We must show ourselves partners in the victory.

The account in the tenth chapter of Joshua shows how Joshua required the Israelites to identify themselves with the position of victors. After a great battle, during which Joshua commanded the sun to stand still, he returned to his Gilgal camp. However, the Bible says, "But these five kings fled, and hid themselves in a cave at Makkedah" (v. 16). Joshua commanded that huge stones be placed at the mouth of the cave to prevent the kings from escaping while the Israelites continued to fight their enemies. Then, returning to the cave, Joshua commanded that the kings be brought before him. The mouth of the cave was opened and the kings of Jerusalem, Hebron, Jarmuth, Lachish and Eglon stood before Joshua. The Bible says, "When they brought out those kings unto Joshua, that Joshua called for all the men of Israel, and said unto the captains of the men of war which went with him, Come near, put your feet upon the necks of these kings. And they came near, and put their feet upon the necks of them. And Joshua said unto them, Fear not, nor be dismayed, be strong and of good courage: for thus shall the Lord do to all your enemies against whom ye fight" (vv. 24,25). The placing of their feet on the necks of their enemies was the symbol of victory for the conquerors of Joshua's day. Joshua required that his captains of war do this to identify themselves in this victory and reminded them that the Lord would give them victory over all their enemies.

We also have a victorious position, which Christ has obtained for us. The fact that God has "raised us up together, and made us sit together in heavenly places in Christ Jesus" (Eph. 2:6) does not mean that we have been physically transported to a heavenly position; rather, by faith we are in this place of victory.

Jesus Christ has completely conquered the enemy, but the enemy will continue to harass us until we take our position of victory with Christ. It is as in a physical battle where the one at the top of the hill has the advantage. Christ is at the top of the hill because He has conquered Satan, and we can be victorious over Satan only as we take our position with Christ.

We must act by faith on the basis of our position in Christ. Beware of those who talk of living by faith as if there is absolutely nothing the believer does. Some give the impression that the believer becomes totally passive and that God does everything apart from the will and personality of the believer. God does accomplish the victory, but He does it in and through the believer. We must not rely on self-effort, but neither are we to be guilty of laziness or disobedience in following the Lord. The Lord does not override our wills, but as we place our faith in Him and live accordingly, He will give us victory. God not only does the work in and through us but He even gives us the desire to do His will: "For it is God who is at work in you, both to will and to work for His good pleasure" (Phil. 2:13, NASB). The preceding verse indicates that we are to work out through our lives what God works in us. This calls for obedience, and only when we are obedient will we be powerful in the Lord.

Source of Confidence

The account of I Samuel 17 illustrates the importance of trusting in the Lord rather than in human resources. This passage of Scripture tells how the giant Goliath and the Philistines were challenging the army of Israel. Goliath bargained with the Israelites to choose a man to fight against him, and the army of the winner would be considered victorious over the other army. No one in the army of Israel was willing to accept the challenge. When young David came looking for his brothers, he learned of Goliath's challenge and offered to fight him himself. At first no one would take David seriously because he was such a young man and Goliath was a veteran of warfare.

David recounted for King Saul how he had killed a lion and a bear while he was keeping his father's sheep, and he was confident that the Lord would deliver Goliath into his hand, just as He had the wild animals. Saul agreed to let David fight Goliath, but before he sent David out he gave him his armor. Trying on Saul's armor, David realized he would be unable to fight Goliath while wearing this armor because he was not used to it. The armor is a reminder of man-made protection in warfare. David's past victories had been because of trust in the Lord, not because of trusting in man-made armor.

Saul was a man of weak faith; his confidence was almost entirely in the armor. David was a man of strong faith; his confidence was in God.

David's confidence in God was evident from what he said to Goliath after he had taken five smooth stones and met Goliath at the place of battle: "Thou comest to me with a sword, and with a spear, and with a shield: but I come to thee in the name of the Lord of hosts, the God of the armies of Israel, whom thou hast defied. This day will the Lord deliver thee into mine hand" (vv. 45,46). David told Goliath that all of this was to be so "that all the earth may know that there is a God in Israel. And all this assembly shall know that the Lord saveth not with sword and spear: for the battle is the Lord's, and he will give you into our hands" (vv. 46,47).

How could David be so sure? He had learned that confidence in the Lord is never misplaced. In the words of Ephesians 6, David was "strong in the Lord, and in the power of his might" (v. 10).

The great need today is for believers to be "strong in the Lord." This is not a matter of progressive attainment; rather, it is a matter of occupying one's victorious position that Christ has already gained for us. As we recognize these truths and live accordingly, our faith will become more courageous for we will see God work in our lives. But it is important to remember that we need to take our position with Christ before we begin battle. Jesus Christ has already triumphed over our foes; therefore, we need to take our position with Him in the place of victory. Just as there was no question in David's mind before the battle but what God would give the victory, there should be no question in the believer's mind because Christ has already accomplished the victory. The real victory over Goliath was won before David ever went to meet him in the valley; our victory in spiritual warfare has been won by Christ before we enter the battle.

The conflict does not consist in fighting *for* a victory with the Lord's help. We do not need to ask the Lord to help us to gain a victory, since He has already gained the victory. We do not fight *for* victory but *from* a position of victory in Christ. This is the character of our spiritual conflict. Because Christ has already accomplished the victory, the enemy has already been dislodged from his stronghold and is a conquered foe (Heb. 2:14; Col. 2:15).

The Lord Is Our Strength

Not only has the Lord accomplished the victory for us, but He also indwells and strengthens us. Because He indwells us, it is more than our getting our strength from Him; it is that He Himself *is* our strength.

The Bible indicates the believer is in a place of victory and that his responsibility is to hold his position, not to attempt to gain it. Ephesians 6:11,13 emphasizes that we are to "stand" and "withstand." This is holding our position in Christ.

Revelation 2:25,26 provide an illustration of this. To the Church of Thyatira, the Lord Jesus Christ said, "But that which ye have already hold fast till I come. And he that overcometh, and keepeth my works unto the end, to him will I give power over the nations." Here we see that to overcome is to maintain one's position. The Lord Jesus Christ told the Church at Philadelphia, "Behold, I come quickly: hold that fast which thou hast, that no man take thy crown. Him that overcometh will I make a pillar in the temple of my God" (3:11,12). There is no substitute for the strength and power that is ours because of our position in Christ. From Ephesians 6 we see that the believer is made fit with inner strength before he is offered outer equipment, or armor. This armor is valuable only as our minds and wills are properly adjusted by our faith relationship to the Lord Jesus Christ.

Ephesians 6:10 says, "Be strong in the Lord, and in the power of his might." The words "be strong" can be translated "be strengthened." Here Paul used the Greek present tense so it has the meaning of "be continually strengthened." First Corinthians 16:13 says, "Be on the alert, stand firm in the faith, act like men, be strong" (NASB).

Ephesians 6:10 contains three Greek words that emphasize different aspects of power, or strength. The word translated "be strong" means "to make strong, to endue with strength." It portrays a person clothing himself with strength as one puts on a garment. As we have seen, it is used in a tense which emphasizes continuous action. Also notice that it is a command—for us to "be strong in the Lord."

The word translated "power" refers to manifested power. This word was often used of a power that depends on another's power—in this case it is the believer's power that depends on the power of Christ.

The word translated "might" refers to a special enduement of power. The believer is endued with power from Christ, and because Christ lives in the believer, He really is the believer's power. Colossians 1:27 refers to this when it says, "Christ in you, the hope of glory." Verse 29 says, "For this I labor [unto weariness], striving with all the superhuman energy which He so mightily enkindles and works within me" (Amplified). This refers to the same power mentioned in Ephesians 1:19: "The exceeding greatness of his power to us-ward who believe, according to the working of his mighty power."

Chapter 3

The Believer's Foes and Their Methods
(Eph. 6:11,12,16)

The primary foe of believers is referred to in Ephesians 6:11, which records Paul's command, "Put on the whole armour of God, that ye may be able to stand against the wiles of the devil." The Devil himself, also known as "Satan," is the believer's main enemy.

From this we see that even though the world system and the flesh are enemies of the believer, the key figure in the spiritual confict that the believer must face is Satan. So the conflict of Ephesians 6 does not come from within but from without the believer. Paul gave instructions earlier in Ephesians as to how the internal enemy of the flesh was to be dealt with. These instructions were given specifically in 4:22-24, where we were told to put off the things related to the old nature and to put on those things becoming to the new nature. If we have done what Paul said to do, we can treat self, or the flesh, as a conquered foe. However, we must remember that the desires of the old nature continually seek our attention so we must always be on our guard concerning the flesh.

Having been faithful in overcoming the internal foe, we now can turn our attention toward overcoming the external foe. If, however, we have not come to grips with the problem of self, we are in no position to maintain victory over Satan. The Old Testament Israelites serve as a national parallel to this individual problem. After the Israelites were delivered from Egypt, they wandered in the desert, being preoccupied with themselves and murmuring against God. During the years of wandering they were ineffective for God because they refused to take Him at His word and go into Canaan and conquer the land. The older generation died in the wilderness because of their disobedience, but the new generation believed God, left the desert behind them and entered the land God had promised to them. There they engaged in warfare against God's and their common enemies, for even though God had promised them the land they had to act on faith and take it. They were able to effectively stand against their enemies only as they overcame preoccupation with themselves.

So, too, Satan has no need to attack us as long as we are preoccupied with self. However, when we take God at His word and walk by faith, we can be sure that we will be exposed to and experience the attacks of Satan. Of course, the believer can avoid much spiritual conflict by remaining in a spiritual desert even as Israel remained in the desert rather than believing God and engaging in warfare. But if the believer fails to move out for the Lord he will never know the joy of spiritual victory the Lord desires him to know. There may be conflict but it will be the conflict of the believer's will with God's will, not the spiritual conflict that is referred to in Ephesians 6.

The warfare described in Ephesians 6:10-20 is a warfare in which we join the Lord in holding the position of victory that He has already secured. We need not yield to fear concerning Satan for Christ has been victorious over him and our need is to claim our position of victory in Christ.

Binding the Strong Man

Matthew 12:28-30 gives us a lesson in spiritual warfare. The Lord Jesus Christ was accused of casting out demons by the power of Satan, but He answered, "If I cast out devils [demons] by the Spirit of God, then the kingdom of God is come unto you. Or how else can one enter into a strong man's house, and spoil his goods, except he first bind the strong man? and then he will spoil his house. He that is not with me is against me; and he that gathereth not with me scattereth abroad." The Lord Jesus was telling the Pharisees that the reason He was able to cast out demons was because He had power over Satan himself. Jesus' statement "He that is not with me is against me" (v. 30) refers to our refusing to take our position with Christ in binding Satan. After Jesus Christ died for our sin He was buried, rose from the dead and ascended to the Heavenly Father. He won the victory over Satan and provided salvation for the entire world. Those of us who trust in Him as Saviour become part of His mystical Body, the Church. Those who have not yet believed are in a sense bound by Satan because they have been blinded by him (II Cor. 4:3,4). Our responsibility as believers is to pray for these who are blinded by Satan, for in this way we engage in spiritual warfare and stand with Christ in overcoming Satan; that is, in binding the strong man (Matt. 12:29).

Notice that there is no neutral position—people are either for Christ or against Him (Matt. 12:30). It is impossible to maintain a middle-of-the-road position concerning one's relationship with Jesus Christ.

Even as God promised the land of Canaan to Joshua and the Israelites but required them to personally take the land, so Christ has gained the victory over Satan but requires us to take our position with Him in praying for those who are bound by him. By prayer, we loose them from Satan's power and gather them for Christ.

After the Israelites had been in the land a few years, they still had not possessed the land. Joshua said to them, "How long are ye slack to go to possess the land, which the Lord God of your fathers hath given you?" (Josh. 18:3). So, too, the Lord must wonder why some believers today are so hesitant to identify themselves with Him in victory over Satan and to engage in spiritual warfare to see others come to Christ.

Our warfare is not primarily with other persons but with Satan. Ephesians 6:11 says that we're to stand "against the wiles of the devil," and verse 12 reminds us that we are not in conflict against "flesh and blood." The real enemy is not visible; he is a mighty but unseen foe. However, he expresses himself through that which is visible, whether it be people or circumstances. He presents temptations to believers, hoping they will yield to them and discredit Christ. We are warring not only against Satan, but also against his hosts, for verse 12 says we're warring against "principalities, against powers, against the rulers of the darkness of this world, against spiritual wickedness in high places." Man-made weapons are of no advantage in this spiritual warfare. Man-made weapons are weapons of the flesh, but II Corinthians 10:3-5 reminds us, "For though we walk in the flesh, we do not war after the flesh: (for the weapons of our warfare are not carnal, but mighty through God to the pulling down of strong holds;) casting down imaginations, and every high thing that exalteth itself against the knowledge of God, and bringing into captivity every thought to the obedience of Christ."

The hosts of Satan are fallen angels who do his bidding. Although Satan is not omnipresent, his will is carried out on a universal scale through his emissaries. He is their commander in chief. This host of fallen angels are referred to as principalities and powers in Ephesians 6:12. This indicates that the messengers of Satan are a well-organized army divided into ranks and divisions. "Principalities" is literally "rulers," and "powers" is literally "authorities." Thus, principalities and powers refer to the supremacy of rule and authority in the satanic realm. The words "rulers of the darkness of this world" is literally "the world rulers of this darkness." No wonder it is said that our warfare is "against spiritual wickedness in high places" (v. 12).

The Greek word translated "high places" in Ephesians 6:12 is the same word that is translated "heavenly places" in 1:3,20; 2:6 and 3:10. Although the heavenly realm is referred to in both instances, a different sphere of heaven is intended. From II Corinthians 12:2 we learn that there are three heavens, for Paul referred to a person—probably himself—who was "caught up to the third heaven." The third heaven is the place of God's special abode, the second is the stellar heaven, and the first is the atmospheric heaven, which is closest to earth.

Although principalities and powers are in a heavenly realm, the believer's position with Christ is higher than these, for Ephesians 1:20,21 tells us that the Father set Christ "at his own right hand in the heavenly places, far above all principality, and power, and might, and dominion, and every name that is named, not only in this world, but also in that which is to come." It is the third heaven that Christ referred to as "my Father's house" (John 14:2), and it is there that Christ is seated at the right hand of the Father. It is here that we have our spiritual position with Christ; therefore, *in Him* we too are situated above these satanic forces in spiritual authority. This is our position by faith.

Satan's Dwelling Place

There was a time when Satan—then known as "Lucifer"—lived in the third heaven with God. Isaiah 14:12-14 refers to Satan's fall from the third heaven: "How art thou fallen from heaven, O Lucifer, son of the morning! how art thou cut down to the ground, which didst weaken the nations! For thou hast said in thine heart, I will ascend into heaven, I will exalt my throne above the stars of God: I will sit also upon the mount of the congregation, in the sides of the north: I will ascend above the heights of the clouds; I will be like the most High." Ezekiel 28:14,15 reveals that Lucifer was created without sin: "Thou art the anointed cherub that covereth; and I have set thee so: thou wast upon the holy mountain of God; thou hast walked up and down in the midst of the stones of fire. Thou wast perfect in thy ways from the day that thou wast created, till iniquity was found in thee."

Satan does not dwell in the third heaven although he has access to it to accuse those who have faith in God (see Job 1:6-12; 2:1-7). Having been thrown out of the third heaven, the place of God's abode, Satan now has domain in the first and second heavens—the atmospheric and stellar heavens. He is known as the "prince of the power of the air" (Eph. 2:2).

During the coming Tribulation, Satan and his angels will also be thrown out of the first and second heavens onto the earth. Referring to the battle of Michael and his angels against Satan and his angels, Revelation 12:9 says, "And the great dragon was cast out, that old serpent, called the Devil, and Satan, which deceiveth the whole world: he was cast out into the earth, and his angels were cast out with him." Viewing this time prophetically, the Apostle John said, "And I heard a loud voice saying in heaven, Now is come salvation, and strength, and the kingdom of our God, and the power of his Christ: for the accuser of our brethren is cast down, which accused them before our God day and night" (v. 10). Observe how Satan is overcome when he is thrown down to the earth: "They overcame him by the blood of the Lamb, and by the word of their testimony; and they loved not their lives unto the death" (v. 11). Because Christ fully judged Satan when He shed His blood on the cross, Satan has no power against the benefits of Christ's death or against the Word of God. When Satan and his angels are thrown out of heaven onto the earth, Satan's full fury will be seen "because he knoweth that he hath but a short time" (v. 12). Since these events will take place during the Tribulation, the Church of Jesus Christ will not be on earth, having been raptured before the Tribulation began. This is why verse 12 says, "Therefore rejoice, ye heavens, and ye that dwell in them." These words are said to the Church, who is dwelling in heaven with Christ while the Tribulation is raging on earth.

Know the Enemy

One of the most basic matters in warfare is to know the enemy you are fighting. We cannot expect to be successful in spiritual warfare against Satan if we do not know who he is and what his tactics are.

Even a casual acquaintance with Scripture reveals that Satan is much more than an influence; he is a person, and as such, he speaks, he plans, he deceives, he hates, he fights. Yet some people refuse to believe that the Devil is a real person, maintaining that he is only the influence of evil, or a symbol of evil. Even this misconception is a tribute to Satan's success in deceiving unbelievers. One of his best methods of concealing his activities is to influence people to think that he does not exist. A false optimism appears wherever Satan is not recognized as the key enemy working in human affairs. Satan has been so successful in hiding himself that some people even think they can bring in the millennium by their own good efforts. However, before a millennium of peace is known by the world it will be necessary for Jesus Christ to personally return and confine Satan to the bottomless pit (20:3).

The only way to overcome Satan is to confront him with the finished work of Calvary by which Christ gained the victory over him. Satan knows that he is ultimately a defeated foe because of what Christ accomplished on the cross. We have seen that during the Tribulation believers will overcome Satan by the blood of the Lamb and by their testimony (12:11). This is the same basis for our victory over Satan now, for we cannot be victorious over him on our own—it is only as we claim our position in Christ that we will experience victory.

The Bible has much to say about Satan. The titles it gives to Satan explain his activities. He is called the "prince of the power of the air" (Eph. 2:2), referring to Satan's exercise of power in the atmospheric and stellar heavens. He is also called "the prince of this world" (John 12:31), which reveals that Satan claims the throne of this world. Satan's power over the world is revealed in I John 5:19: "We know that we are of God, and the whole world lies in the power of the evil one" (NASB).

Satan is referred to as "the god of this world" (II Cor. 4:4), which reveals that he claims and accepts the worship of the world. Where the gospel has not been preached, it is common to find the people worshiping Satan and demons out of fear.

He is also referred to as "the accuser of our brethren" (Rev. 12:10), and the first two chapters of Job reveal how he does this. Satan seeks to bring about the ruin of God's children by these accusations. Satan first entices the people of God to sin; then he accuses them before God of the sin they have committed. However, we need have no fear for Jesus Christ stands as our Advocate before the Father: "My little children, these things write I unto you, that ye sin not. And if any man sin, we have an advocate with the Father, Jesus Christ the righteous" (I John 2:1). The Lord Jesus Christ pleads our case as does a lawyer, and the basis for his plea is what He accomplished for us on the cross. The following verse says, "And he is the propitiation [satisfaction] for our sins: and not for our's only, but also for the sins of the whole world."

When we sin we need to confess our sin to God, who has promised to forgive when we confess it: "If we confess our sins, he is faithful and just to forgive us our sins, and to cleanse us from all unrighteousness" (I John 1:9). God's forgiveness is based on the fact that Christ has already paid the penalty for our sin. Thus, when we confess our sin, we are restored to fellowship with the Heavenly Father.

Satan's Methods

When writing to the Corinthians regarding Satan, Paul reminded them, "For we are not ignorant of his devices" (II Cor. 2:11). However, it seems today that believers are frequently ignorant of the methods Satan uses, so let us look at several of them.

From II Corinthians 4:4 we learn that Satan blinds the minds of unbelievers: "In whom the god of this world hath blinded the minds of them which believe not, lest the light of the glorious gospel of Christ, who is the image of God, should shine unto them." Satan wants to keep people from seeing their need to receive Christ as Saviour. Our responsibility in this spiritual warfare is to cooperate with Christ, by prayer, in binding Satan so he will not be able to keep in bondage those he has blinded.

Another tactic of Satan is seen from II Corinthians 11:13-15: "For such are false apostles, deceitful workers, transforming themselves into the apostles of Christ. And no marvel; for Satan himself is transformed into an angel of light. Therefore it is no great thing if his ministers also be transformed as the ministers of righteousness; whose end shall be according to their works." There are many in pulpits today who do not preach the gospel of the grace of Christ; rather, they teach a gospel of works. It sounds reasonable because people like to think they must work for anything that is worth having. Through such teaching Satan has transformed himself into an angel of light that he might keep unbelievers from the kingdom of God.

From Ephesians 2:2 we see that Satan energizes men to disobedience: "Wherein in time past ye walked according to the course of this world, according to the prince of the power of the air, the spirit that now worketh in the children of disobedience."

The main tactic of Satan is to deceive the world. This is evident from Revelation 12:9, where he is referred to as "that old serpent, called the Devil, and Satan, which deceiveth the whole world." Referring to the Antichrist, who will appear during the coming Tribulation, II Thessalonians 2:9 says, "Even him, whose coming is after the working of Satan with all power and signs and lying wonders." By his "lying wonders" he will deceive the world during the Tribulation.

Paul referred to those who were caught in Satan's trap when he told Timothy, "With gentleness correcting those who are in opposition; if perhaps God may grant them repentance, leading to the knowledge of the truth, and they may come to their senses and escape from the snare of the devil, having been held captive by him to do his will" (II Tim. 2:25,26, NASB).

Satan also originates false doctrine to mislead mankind. The Bible says, "Now the Spirit speaketh expressly, that in the latter times some shall depart from the faith, giving heed to seducing spirits, and doctrines of devils [demons]" (I Tim. 4:1). Satan encourages all doctrine that is contrary to the Scriptures because it detracts from Jesus Christ. Liberal theology that denies the deity of Christ, His atoning work on the cross, and His personal return, is inspired by Satan himself.

The power of Satan is closely associated with his methods. Hebrews 2:14 indicates that before Christ's death on the cross, Satan had the "power of death." However, it is evident that even during Old Testament times Satan's power was restricted by God. When Satan wanted to bring affliction on Job, God said, "Behold, all that he hath is in thy power; only upon himself put not forth thine hand" (Job 1:12). Later, God permitted Satan to go further in his testing of Job, but told Satan, "Behold, he is in thine hand; but save his life" (2:6). From these verses we see that Satan was not able to exercise his power beyond the boundaries which God had prescribed.

The believer is able to be victorious over Satan because of his position in Christ and of the effectiveness of his weapons. Since we are seated "together in heavenly places in Christ Jesus" (Eph. 2:6), no one is able to touch us without touching Christ Himself. Paul reminded believers, "For the weapons of our warfare are not carnal, but mighty through God to the pulling down of strong holds" (II Cor. 10:4).

Our position in Christ makes it impossible for Satan to gain the victory over us as long as we remain in our position by faith. Christ has all power over principalities and powers; thus, the believer benefits from this power as he, by faith, utilizes the authority of Christ. Someone has said that the believer is a Christ-enclosed person; that is, Satan cannot touch him apart from touching Christ Himself.

Satan knows where he is defeated. He is too experienced to waste time and strength against walls that he knows are impregnable. So we need not fear Satan's attack as long as we are entrenched in our position in Christ. However, because Satan is cunning, he will attempt to draw us out of our position and cause us to rely on our own strength to defeat him, rather than on the strength we have in Christ.

Ephesians 6:11 refers to the "wiles" of Satan. The word translated "wiles" is the word from which "methods" is derived. As used in Bible times, it referred to cunning arts, deceit, craft, trickery. Satan uses subtle methods to allure us out of our stronghold in Christ. If Satan is able to get the believer to doubt, or even to entertain discouragement (both come from Satan), he has greater hopes of succeeding in his schemes. The moment the believer no longer relies on his faith position in Christ he falls under Satan's power. We need to heed Christ's words, "Watch ye therefore, and pray always" (Luke 21:36).

Paul did not view the Christian life as being easy, and he encouraged Timothy: "Fight the good fight of faith" (I Tim. 6:12). It is in this fight of faith that the believer needs to utilize the armor mentioned in Ephesians 6, which will be discussed in the following chapter. In the spiritual conflict it is important that we not be overconfident and think we can defeat Satan on our own. The Bible instructs believers, "Humble yourselves therefore under the mighty hand of God, that he may exalt you in due time: Casting all your care upon him; for he careth for you. Be sober, be vigilant; because your adversary the devil, as a roaring lion, walketh about, seeking whom he may devour: whom resist stedfast in the faith, knowing that the same afflictions are accomplished in your brethren that are in the world" (I Pet. 5:6-9). First Peter 4:7 says, "The end of all things is at hand: be ye therefore sober, and watch unto prayer."

It is encouraging to remember that the weakest believer who lives on the basis of his faith position in Christ is as safe as the most mature believer because both are within the same impregnable fortress. Such a believer can say with David,

"The Lord is my rock, and my fortress, and my deliverer; the God of my rock; in him will I trust: he is my shield, and the horn of my salvation, my high tower, and my refuge, my saviour; thou savest me from violence. I will call on the Lord, who is worthy to be praised: so shall I be saved from mine enemies" (II Sam. 22:2-4).

It should also be realized that the most advanced believer is weak and helpless the moment he ceases to rely on his position in Christ. It is not necessary for one to constantly think about his position in Christ, but it must be the basis for all that he is and does. It is necessary, therefore, for the believer to come to the point in his life where he recognizes this truth and lives accordingly from that time forward.

Ephesians 6:16 refers to the believer's being able "to quench all the fiery darts of the wicked [one]." These darts are the temptations by which Satan attacks the believer. However, when we are under the attack of some temptation, we should remember the truth of I Corinthians 10:12,13: "Wherefore let him that thinketh he standeth take heed lest he fall. There hath no temptation taken you but such as is common to man: but God is faithful, who will not suffer you to be tempted above that ye are able; but will with the temptation also make a way to escape, that ye may be able to bear it."

When we are under attack by Satan, we will find the Scriptures to be of particular encouragement, for they remind us of God's faithfulness in the time of testing. Several years ago when I was preparing for an overseas trip to take care of important Broadcast business, several told me of their fear that I might not return. The same fear had bothered me to the extent I realized I was doubting God's goodness and sovereignty in my life. After boarding the plane I turned to Psalm 91, which was of tremendous comfort to me at that time. As I read this psalm I was reassured of my position as a believer, and the attack of Satan was warded off. The peace that surpasses all understanding guarded my soul as I traveled, and I was reassured of the wonderful presence of God. Verses 1 and 2 of this great psalm say, "He that dwelleth in the secret place of the most High shall abide under the shadow of the Almighty. I will say of the Lord, He is my refuge and my fortress: my God; in him will I trust"

In this psalm God tells the believer, "Because he hath set his love upon me, therefore will I deliver him: I will set him on high, because he hath known my name. He shall call upon me, and I will answer him: I will be with him in trouble; I will deliver him, and honour him. With long life will I satisfy him, and shew him my salvation" (vv. 14-16). How wonderful and reassuring is God's Word when we are experiencing the fiery darts of the Wicked One!

Chapter 4

The Armor Provided

(Eph. 6:11; 13-17)

Ephesians 6:11 tells us, "Put on the whole armour of God, that ye may be able to stand against the wiles of the devil." Verse 13 says, "Wherefore take unto you the whole armour of God, that ye may be able to withstand in the evil day, and having done all, to stand." The words "whole armour" occur in both verses. Every piece of the spiritual armor is needed because of the nature of the conflict as described in verses 11 and 12. We are fighting against the "wiles of the devil" and "we wrestle not against flesh and blood, but against principalities, against powers, against the rulers of the darkness of this world, against spiritual wickedness in high places."

The whole armor of God that the believer is to take upon himself enables him to ward off the attacks of Satan. The provisions for living the abundant life are really centered in the second and third Persons of the Godhead—the Lord Jesus Christ and the Holy Spirit. Since the Holy Spirit's ministry is to reveal to the believer the things of Christ (John 16:14,15), the attention of the believer is to be focused especially on the Person of Christ. When this is so, it indicates the believer has been sensitive to the ministry of the Spirit, who seeks to direct attention to Jesus Christ. The Book of Ephesians emphasizes the Lord Jesus Christ, but it presupposes the ministry of the indwelling Holy Spirit.

Having been raised to sit in heavenly places "in Christ" (Eph. 2:6), we need to appropriate what Christ has provided that we might live abundantly. Jesus Christ has made available to us everything we need to enable us to victoriously stand against the Enemy. However, our position must be occupied by faith; that is, our trust must be in Christ to do and provide what He has said.

Notice that Ephesians 6:11,13,14 uses the word "stand" in telling of our conflict with the Enemy. We are not to run but to stand. Too many seem to think that they can somehow outrun the foe, or they think that if they can at least stay a few steps ahead of him, they will be able to live abundantly. However, we are not called to a spiritual marathon; we are called to take a firm stand until the foe is doing the running. This is why James 4:7 says, "Submit yourselves therefore to God. Resist the devil, and he will flee from you." Notice that before we can successfully resist Satan we must submit ourselves to God.

First Peter 5:9 also reveals that the believer's position is not one of fleeing but resisting: "Whom [Satan] resist stedfast in the faith." As has been indicated, we withstand Satan now in the same way that believers will withstand him during the Tribulation: "They overcame him by the blood of the Lamb, and by the word of their testimony; and they loved not their lives unto the death" (Rev. 12:11).

As we take our position in Christ, we will be "strong in the Lord, and in the power of his might" (Eph. 6:10). This submitting to God involves the reckoning and yielding of Romans 6:11-13.

Notice that we are to "take" the whole armor of God (Eph. 6:13). God has already provided the armor; our need is to appropriate what He has made available. Just as God promised the land of Canaan to the Israelites but still required them to actually take the land (Josh. 1:3), so God has promised victory for believers but requires us to take up the armor and stand victorious.

Concerning verse 13 and the significance of the words "take unto you," a Greek scholar, Kenneth S. Wuest, has written: " 'Take unto you' is *analambano*, 'to take up' in order to use. . . . The verb is aorist imperative, which construction issues a command given with military snap and curtness, a command to be obeyed at once, and once for all. Thus, the Christian is to take up and put on all the armor of God as a once-for-all act and keep that armor on during the entire course of his life, not relaxing the discipline necessary for the constant use of such protection" (*Word Studies in the Greek New Testament*, p. 142).

Thus we see that the armor is not to be put on and taken off periodically but to be put on and left on. The armor is actually an attitude of faith; therefore, it is something that is put on by an act of the will and left on. As we mature in the Christian life, we will discover areas in our lives where our faith is not as strong as it should be; that is, the armor is weak in a certain place. At such a time, our responsibility is to go to the Word of God to study His promises concerning our area of weakness, so that our faith will be strengthened. The putting on of the armor once for all is well illustrated by the words of Romans 12:1,2: "I beseech you therefore, brethren, by the mercies of God, that ye present your bodies a living sacrifice, holy, acceptable unto God, which is your reasonable service. And be not conformed to this world: but be ye transformed by the renewing of your mind, that ye may prove what is that good, and acceptable, and perfect, will of God." There is to be a once-for-all presenting of the body to God, followed by a maturing attitude of heart and mind as we grow in the knowledge of Him.

Notice the parallel between Ephesians 6:11, "Put on the whole armour of God," and Romans 13:14, "Put ye on the Lord Jesus Christ." God's provision for victory is in the Person of the Lord Jesus Christ and through the Word of God.

In putting on the Lord Jesus Christ, we need to remember that the living Word (Jesus Christ) is revealed through the written Word (the Bible). In His prayer for His own, Jesus prayed, "Sanctify them through thy truth: thy word is truth" (John 17:17). We put on the Lord Jesus Christ as we study the Word of God and obey what it says.

The believer's armor, then, is not physical protective equipment but is Jesus Christ Himself. Putting on Christ is similar to what we are told in Ephesians 4:24: "Put on the new man." This new man is Christ formed in the believer. Paul was greatly concerned that this be true of every believer, and he told the Galatians: "I travail in birth again until Christ be formed in you" (4:19). Christ was being formed in Paul's life, and this was why he could say, "I am crucified with

Christ: nevertheless I live; yet not I, but Christ liveth in me"
(2:20).

As we have seen from Ephesians 6:11-13 the emphasis is
on the whole armor; it is not sufficient to take on only part
of the armor. The Enemy strikes the believer at his most
vulnerable point so it is imperative that he have the full
armor. Just as some people are susceptible to certain diseases,
some believers are susceptible to certain attacks of Satan.
However, the only assurance of effectiveness against all
attacks is to take on the whole armor. The whole armor
includes the girdle of truth and the breastplate of
righteousness (v. 14); shoes (v. 15); the shield of faith (v. 16);
the helmet of salvation and the sword of the Spirit (v. 17).

Observe that the whole armor is for the whole body. God
has provided the armor primarily to protect the most
precious thing He has on earth—the mystical Body of His
Son, which we are.

The armor is defensive in its entirety. Even the sword of
the Spirit is mentioned here for defense against Satan's
attacks, just as Jesus used the Word when attacked by Satan
(Matt. 4:4,7,10). Although the Word of God is used
offensively at other times, here the emphasis is on its
defensive use.

As has been mentioned, the armor has been given so that
we may be able to stand our ground against Satan. But the
victory is not a once-for-all victory. Having stood our ground
victoriously, Satan will attack us from a different angle or
wait for a time when we do not have our armor in its proper
place. Satan is not easily discouraged so we must watch his
persistent attacks and not become lax after we have
experienced a victory. We must keep right on standing in our
victorious position. Peter says that the Devil is going about
"as a roaring lion . . . seeking whom he may devour" (I Pet.
5:8). He is looking for someone who is off guard. Our
responsibility is to "resist stedfast in the faith" (v. 9).

As we resist by faith, we may be confident that God will
keep us in victory. Paul said, "But thanks be to God, which
giveth us the victory through our Lord Jesus Christ.
Therefore, my beloved brethren, be ye stedfast, unmoveable,
always abounding in the work of the Lord, for as much as ye

know that your labour is not in vain in the Lord" (I Cor. 15:57,58).

We are to stand against the wiles of the Devil and then go forward in service for Christ. Although Satan may roar as a lion, the noise he makes need have no terror for us. Since Satan realizes his time is limited he becomes more vicious in his attacks, but he is unable to harm the believer who is totally submitted to Christ. Satan is the one who must run and leave his position of control in the field of battle, for Satan is a defeated foe (Heb. 2:14).

There is no need for the believer to fear that Satan will attack him as if in the dark. Under the attack of the Enemy we can say with David, "Yea, though I walk through the valley of the shadow of death, I will fear no evil: for thou art with me; thy rod and thy staff they comfort me. Thou preparest a table before me in the presence of mine enemies: thou anointest mine head with oil; my cup runneth over" (Ps. 23:4,5).

The key words for believers are "watch" and "pray." We are to watch for Satan's attacks which we will discern as we study the Word of God. We are also to pray for wisdom and enablement in resisting the attacks of Satan. By watching the Word and praying in the Spirit we can remain in the fortress that allows us to stand victorious against Satan.

Having put Christ on as the armor, we do not need to fearfully look around to see if Satan is lurking someplace to attack us. Satan is not able to affect us without first affecting Christ, so our need is to keep "looking unto Jesus the author and finisher of our faith" (Heb. 12:2). When we take our eyes off Christ we leave ourselves open for attack.

Remember Peter who wanted to walk out on the water to meet the Lord? The Lord invited him to come, and the Bible says, "And when Peter was come down out of the ship, he walked on the water, to go to Jesus. But when he saw the wind boisterous, he was afraid; and beginning to sink, he cried, saying, Lord, save me. And immediately Jesus stretched forth his hand, and caught him, and said unto him, O thou of little faith, wherefore didst thou doubt?" (Matt. 14:29-31). Peter began to sink after he took his eyes off Jesus and began looking around him at the circumstances. So also, we leave ourselves open for attack from Satan when we

take our eyes off Jesus. The Lord Jesus is concerned that
Satan will not take advantage of the believer. At one time,
Jesus told Peter, "Satan hath desired to have you, that he
may sift you as wheat: but I have prayed for thee, that thy
faith fail not" (Luke 22:31,32). Even Satan recognized that
God makes a hedge around His own, for Satan said to God
about Job: "Hast not thou made an hedge about him, and
about his house, and about all that he hath on every side?
thou hast blessed the work of his hands, and his substance is
increased in the land" (Job 1:10).

Read some of the psalms and notice how the psalmist had
confidence in God in face of the enemy. The psalmist said, "I
will lift up my eyes to the mountains; from whence shall my
help come? My help comes from the Lord, who made heaven
and earth" (121:1,2, NASB). The psalmist took comfort in
the fact that his God had made the heaven and the earth;
therefore, God would certainly be able to deliver him from
any difficulty he faced. Thus, he went on to say, "He will not
allow your foot to slip; He who keeps you will not slumber.
Behold, He who keeps Israel will neither slumber nor sleep.
The Lord is your keeper; the Lord is your shade on your
right hand. The sun will not smite you by day, nor the moon
by night. The Lord will protect you from all evil; He will
keep your soul. The Lord will guard your going out and your
coming in from this time forth and forever" (vv. 3-8, NASB).

After the Lord had delivered David from his enemies,
David wrote: "I love Thee, O Lord, my strength. The Lord is
my rock and my fortress and my deliverer, my God, my rock,
in whom I take refuge; my shield and the horn of my
salvation, my stronghold. I call upon the Lord, who is worthy
to be praised, and I am saved from my enemies" (18:1-3,
NASB).

In another psalm, David said, "The steps of a man are
established by the Lord; and He delights in his way. When he
falls, he shall not be hurled headlong; because the Lord is the
One who holds his hand" (37:23,24, NASB). These verses
from the various psalms show the confidence David had in
God. And we can have this same confidence as we
"take . . . the whole armour of God" (Eph. 6:13).

Chapter 5

The Armor Described

(Eph. 6:14-17)

Having told believers to "put on" (Eph. 6:11) and "take" (v. 13) the whole armor of God, Paul then described the armor in verses 14-17.

Girdle of Truth

The first part of armor mentioned is the girdle of truth: "Stand therefore, having your loins girt about with truth" (v. 14).

Concerning truth, Jesus Christ said, "I am the way, the truth, and the life" (John 14:6). Since Jesus Christ is the personification of truth, to put on the girdle of truth is to "put . . . on the Lord Jesus Christ" (Rom. 13:14). Because He is God, Jesus Christ is the embodiment of all truth.

Not only is Jesus Christ the truth, but the Word of God is also truth. Concerning His own, Jesus asked the Father: "Sanctify them through thy truth: thy word is truth" (John 17:17). Christ is the Living Word and the Bible is the written Word, and these together form the believer's girdle of truth.

If we want to be protected against the attacks of the Evil One, we must know Jesus Christ as Saviour and be faithful students of the Word of God. The written Word directs our attention to the Living Word. The better we really know the Scriptures, the more we will want to please God in everything we do.

The psalmist said, "Thy word have I hid in mine heart, that I might not sin against thee" (119:11). This shows us the effect of the Word in a believer's life. Hebrews 4:12 says, "For the word of God is quick [living], and powerful, and

39

sharper than any twoedged sword, piercing even to the dividing asunder of soul and spirit, and of the joints and marrow, and is a discerner of the thoughts and intents of the heart."

The Living Word and the written Word are the power of God. Our desire should be the same as Paul's, which was to know Jesus Christ "and the power of his resurrection" (Phil. 3:10). The power of God is referred to in several Scriptures. Paul said, "For I am not ashamed of the gospel of Christ: for it is the power of God unto salvation to every one that believeth; to the Jew first, and also to the Greek" (Rom. 1:16). First Corinthians 1:24 says, "But unto them which are called, both Jews and Greeks, Christ the power of God, and the wisdom of God." Paul wrote: "But in all things approving ourselves as the ministers of God . . . by the word of truth, by the power of God, by the armour of righteousness on the right hand and on the left" (II Cor. 6:4-7).

To have our "loins girt about with truth" is to have the Living and the written Word controlling our lives. The believer who loves the truth and lives it will have strong spiritual life. Such a person will not be "carried about with every wind of doctrine, by the sleight of men, and cunning craftiness, whereby they lie in wait to deceive" (Eph. 4:14). As Paul wrote to believers about the spiritual armor, he was writing from prison and was perhaps even at that time chained to a Roman soldier. The soldier's belt was not just an adornment; rather, it was to keep various parts of his clothing tightly in place so that he could have total freedom of movement in battle. For the believer to be girded with truth means that he is to have the Living and written Word in his heart and thus be able to meet the onslaughts of Satan.

Breastplate of Righteousness

The second part of the armor to which Paul referred was the "breastplate of righteousness" (Eph. 6:14). The breastplate was worn by the Roman soldier on the upper part of his body and covered both his front and his back. As such, it provided protection for the vital organs of his body.

To Paul, this literal breastplate represented a spiritual breastplate that each believer should use. This spiritual breastplate is an aspect of Christ's protection for the believer against the schemes of the Devil. Just as the literal breastplate protected the soldier's heart, so the spiritual breastplate protects the believer's heart. The Scriptures view the heart as the seat of the emotions, and Satan attacks the believer's emotions to draw his affections and desires away from Christ to the things of this world. The believer is protected from such attacks only as he, by faith, relies on the righteousness of Christ as his breastplate.

We need to remember that our right standing with God is only because of the righteousness of Jesus Christ. The Bible says, "But of him are ye in Christ Jesus, who of God is made unto us wisdom, and righteousness, and sanctification, and redemption" (I Cor. 1:30). Jesus Christ is made "righteousness" to the believer.

That our standing before God is based on His righteousness, not ours, is also seen from Romans 4:5: "But to him that worketh not, but believeth on him that justifieth the ungodly, his faith is counted for righteousness." It is this imputed righteousness of Christ—righteousness placed on our account when we receive Him as Saviour—that cannot be attacked by Satan. This righteousness alone is wound-proof—the darts of Satan cannot pierce it because it is the righteousness of Christ placed to our account. Regardless of Satan's accusations against us before God, we need not fear losing our position in Christ because we are accepted by God because of Christ's righteousness, not because of our own. However, we can be sure that Satan will attack us on the basis of our behavior, and will tempt us to believe that we have lost our standing with God. But Satan's attacks will not be effective if we stand by faith on what the written Word says and let it assure us of our position before God.

If we fail in the Christian life—and we will fail at times—our position in Christ does not change. The reason for this is that our position is not based on the good we have done, or even on our obedience—it is based on what Christ has done. It is for this reason that Satan's accusations, although at times well-grounded because of our behavior, cannot move us from God's presence because we stand there in Christ's righteousness. Christ is our advocate before the Father, and He pleads our case righteously as mentioned in

I John 2:1,2: "My little children, these things write I unto you, that ye sin not. And if any man sin, we have an advocate with the Father, Jesus Christ the righteous: and he is the propitiation for our sins: and not for our's only, but also for the sins of the whole world."

Many believers do not realize that Christ's righteousness is the basis of their security. Those who do not understand this become introspective and discouraged in their Christian life, and lay themselves open to Satan's attacks. Satan is always looking for opportunities to attack a believer. When Satan sees one who has sinned and who is greatly depressed because of his sin, Satan will take advantage of that believer and will bring him even further discouragement. Some become so depressed they even believe they have committed the unpardonable sin, not realizing that the Christian cannot commit such a sin, for all his sins were pardoned when he received Christ as Saviour.

We should once and for all put on the breastplate of righteousness; that is, by faith we should rely on our position in Christ. But it is not enough to know the doctrine; the doctrine must be put into practice. Ephesians 4:24 tells us: "And that ye put on the new man, which after God is created in righteousness and true holiness." We are also told: "For we are his workmanship, created in Christ Jesus unto good works, which God hath before ordained that we should walk in them" (2:10). We must not forget that we were created new for the purpose of good works, so those of us who know Christ should do good and bring glory to Him.

One of Satan's master tricks for those who know of their safety in Christ is to cause them to think that they have no obligation to do good. It is not pleasing to the Lord if we live a worldly, indifferent Christian life, and then put our conscience to sleep by saying something like: "Before God, I am righteous in Christ. What else do I need?" Paul's words answer this type of thinking: "What shall we say then? Shall we continue in sin, that grace may abound? God forbid" (Rom. 6:1,2). Since our standing is righteous in Christ, our practice should be right-doing. Christ is our righteousness for salvation, and He is also our life for our daily right living.

Our position in Christ should be reflected in the way we live. This was the evident desire of Paul's life, as seen from his words: "According to my earnest expectation and my hope, that in nothing I shall be ashamed, but that with all boldness, as always, so now also Christ shall be magnified in my body, whether it be by life, or by death. For to me to live is Christ, and to die is gain" (Phil. 1:20,21). This is why he also said: "I am crucified with Christ: nevertheless I live; yet not I, but Christ liveth in me" (Gal. 2:20). Christ is our righteousness as far as our standing before God is concerned, and He also lives in us to produce His righteousness in our daily lives.

Let us be careful about presuming upon the grace of God. If we are not concerned about glorifying Christ in our daily walk, we may force God to set us aside and to severely chasten us to bring us to our spiritual senses. Paul gave instructions to the Corinthian church concerning what to do about an incorrigible individual. Paul said for them "to deliver such an one unto Satan for the destruction of the flesh, that the spirit may be saved in the day of the Lord Jesus" (I Cor. 5:5). Paul also referred to those believers who will not be rewarded when they stand before the Lord: "If any man's work shall be burned, he shall suffer loss: but he himself shall be saved; yet so as by fire" (3:15). Such an individual, although a believer, has not allowed Christ to work in and through his life so there is no reward for him at the Judgment Seat of Christ (see also II Cor. 5:10).

So let us put on the breastplate of righteousness both as to our position in Christ and as to our practice in our daily walk, and thereby we will defeat Satan.

Shod Feet

The third piece of armor Paul mentioned in Ephesians 6 has to do with the believer's feet: "And your feet shod with the preparation of the gospel of peace" (v. 15). This verse is usually interpreted to mean that the believer is to be prepared to preach the gospel of peace. Romans 10:15 is often cited as a parallel passage: "How beautiful are the feet of them that preach the gospel of peace, and bring glad tidings of good things!"

However, it is my opinion that Ephesians 6:15 refers to having the "message of peace" in our hearts rather than "preaching" the message of peace. This is more in keeping with the context. In the spiritual warfare, Satan is out to destroy the peace in our hearts. He causes us to doubt and fret so that we are in turmoil of soul, thus part of the armor is to give us a settled walk that is peaceful. Ephesians 2:14 tells us that Christ "is our peace."

Many other Scriptures speak of peace. John 14:27 records the words of Jesus: "Peace I leave with you, my peace I give unto you: not as the world giveth, give I unto you. Let not your heart be troubled, neither let it be afraid." Jesus also said, "These things I have spoken unto you, that in me ye might have peace. In the world ye shall have tribulation: but be of good cheer; I have overcome the world" (16:33). Thus, we see that Christ is peace itself. When we possess Him we have true peace, for turmoil of soul disappears.

There are two kinds of peace spoken of in the New Testament—peace *with* God and the peace *of* God. Romans 5:1 refers to peace *with* God: "Therefore being justified by faith, we have peace with God through our Lord Jesus Christ." This kind of peace comes when we turn from our sin and receive Jesus Christ as Saviour. At that moment of decision we become children of God. Because Christ has paid the penalty for our sin, the moment we receive Him as Saviour we are at peace with God. Second Corinthians 5:18 tells us that God has "reconciled us to himself by Jesus Christ." Peace with God is also referred to in Acts 10:36: "The word which God sent unto the children of Israel, preaching peace by Jesus Christ." Christ has thus secured our peace with God inasmuch as this peace is obtained by receiving Him as Saviour. It is a permanent and settled relationship of peace with God that Satan's darts cannot disturb.

The Scriptures also refer to the peace *of* God. Philippians 4:6,7 refers to this kind of peace: "Be careful for nothing; but in every thing by prayer and supplication with thanksgiving let your requests be made known unto God. And the peace of God, which passeth all understanding, shall keep your hearts and minds through Christ Jesus."

Whereas peace with God is a judicial peace in that we are made right with God by receiving Christ as Saviour, the peace of God is an experiential peace. The life of believers is in great contrast to the life of unbelievers. Isaiah said, "But the wicked are like the troubled sea, when it cannot rest, whose waters cast up mire and dirt. There is no peace, saith my God, to the wicked" (57:20,21). Since unbelievers are not at peace with God it is not possible for them to experience the peace of God.

Consider the kind of peace God has. Nothing is able to upset or disturb Him. It is this kind of peace we can experience as we trust Him completely for everything.

Jesus wants His people to have this peace. On the Isle of Patmos, when John was given a revelation of Jesus Christ, John said, "When I saw him, I fell at his feet as dead. And he laid his right hand upon me, saying unto me, Fear not; I am the first and the last: I am he that liveth, and was dead; and, behold, I am alive for evermore, Amen; and have the keys of hell and of death" (Rev. 1:17,18). Jesus also said of Himself: "I am Alpha and Omega, the beginning and the ending . . . which is, and which was, and which is to come, the Almighty" (1:8). As we read these words concerning Christ we see His omnipotence and realize nothing or no one is able to defeat His program. He is allowing certain things to happen on earth now that go against His desires, but eventually Jesus Christ Himself will return to earth to establish His kingdom. He is not frustrated by the events that are now happening. Neither should the believer be frustrated by them, even though he is not able to understand them. If we could only see the future as God sees it, we would have no questions, but God has intended that we walk by faith instead of by sight.

We will experience the peace of God as we realize the security we have in Him. Jesus said, "My sheep hear my voice, and I know them, and they follow me: and I give unto them eternal life; and they shall never perish, neither shall any man pluck them out of my hand. My Father, which gave them me, is greater than all; and no man is able to pluck them out of my Father's hand" (John 10:27-29). So when Paul told believers that their feet should be "shod with the preparation of the gospel of peace" he was referring to the peace with God and peace of God that is possible for everyone who knows Christ as Saviour. Christ died so that we could have peace with God and its resulting peace of God, and through the Holy Spirit this peace is maintained in our hearts.

The question might be asked concerning Ephesians 6:15: Why are the feet mentioned in connection with this peace? The significance lies in the fact that feet are symbolic of our daily walk, or life. The Lord Jesus Christ is presented here as God's provision of peace for daily living. In the process of daily living, there are many circumstances that give rise to fear. In fact, fear is one of the chief characteristics of the last days. Describing these last days, Jesus said, "Men's hearts failing them for fear, and for looking after those things which are coming on the earth: for the powers of heaven shall be shaken" (Luke 21:26). The problems of fear and anxiety plague people the world over, and much study has been given to these subjects. However, the person who has peace through Jesus Christ does not need to fear or to be anxious. Although we do not understand how events will turn out, we are to put all of our care on God, because He cares for us (I Pet. 5:7).

The word in Ephesians 6:15 translated "preparation" means "readiness." However, concerning this word, M. R. Vincent points out that "in Hellenistic Greek it was sometimes used in the sense of the *establishment* or *firm foundation*, which would suit this passage: *firm-footing*" (*Word Studies in the New Testament*, p. 867). So with this solid footing of peace, we can publish the gospel of peace in a world of conflict and evil.

With this deep-seated peace, we can face the foe on every side with true confidence. The psalmist must have experienced this confidence, for he wrote: "It is vain for you to rise up early, to sit up late, to eat the bread of sorrows: for so he giveth his beloved sleep" (127:2). The psalmist also wrote: "Great peace have they which love thy law: and nothing shall offend them" (119:165).

We need to learn to live a day at a time; we should claim for each day God's victory over tension and worry. We should commit the problems of the future to the Lord, because only He knows what the future holds. Jesus spoke of the necessity of believers to have total reliance on Him each day. He said, "Take no thought for your life, what ye shall eat, or what ye shall drink; nor yet for your body, what ye shall put on. Is not the life more than meat, and the body more than raiment?" (Matt. 6:25). Jesus did not mean that we were to make no plans for the future, but we are not to worry about the future over which we have no control.

Jesus further said, "Therefore take no thought, saying, What shall we eat? or, What shall we drink? or, Wherewithal shall we be clothed? (For after all these things do the Gentiles seek:) for your heavenly Father knoweth that ye have need of all these things. But seek ye first the kingdom of God, and his righteousness; and all these things shall be added unto you. Take therefore no thought for the morrow: for the morrow shall take thought for the things of itself. Sufficient unto the day is the evil thereof" (vv. 31-34). To take "thought for the morrow" (v. 34) is to worry about the future, which Jesus says the believer should not do.

David saw the need of trusting the Lord for everything, thus he wrote: "Cast thy burden upon the Lord, and he shall sustain thee: he shall never suffer the righteous to be moved" (Ps. 55:22).

Shield of Faith

The fourth part of the armor for the believer is the "shield of faith." The Bible says, "Above all, taking the shield of faith, wherewith ye shall be able to quench all the fiery darts of the wicked" (Eph. 6:16). "The wicked" is literally "the wicked one" and refers to Satan. Notice the two "alls" in this verse: "Above all" and "all the fiery darts."

"Above all" shows the shield of faith to be of greatest importance. The shield was protection for the entire body. The believer's spiritual shield also protects every aspect of his being.

The shield of faith refers to the Lord Jesus Christ who is God's provision for our protection. It is through faith in Jesus Christ that we are completely protected against the attacks of Satan. The basis of our overcoming in the spiritual warfare is our faith in Christ. The Bible says, "For whatsoever is born of God overcometh the world: and this is the victory that overcometh the world, even our faith. Who is he that overcometh the world, but he that believeth that Jesus is the Son of God?" (I John 5:4,5). We are overcomers because of our faith in Jesus Christ who is "the author and finisher of our faith" (Heb. 12:2).

There is an incident in the Old Testament that provides an interesting parallel to the believer's shield of faith mentioned in Ephesians 6:16. Abraham, then known as "Abram," led 318 of his servants into battle against four kings and their armies in order to rescue Lot, Abraham's nephew. Against such odds, Abraham's victory over the kings was possible only by God's enablement. Abraham and his servants won the victory, and on their return the king of Sodom suggested they keep the spoil of victory. However, Abraham said to him, "I will not take from a thread even to a shoelatchet, and that I will not take any thing that is thine, lest thou shouldest say, I have made Abram rich" (Gen. 14:23). After this victory, Abraham was in great danger of the enemy returning, and he needed protection. This God promised him as seen in Genesis 15:1: "Fear not, Abram: I am thy shield, and thy exceeding great reward." Notice that God did not tell Abraham to "take thy shield" but told him "I am thy shield." God was thereby promising to be Abraham's protector because of Abraham's faith in God.

The psalmist spoke of the Lord as his shield: "Our soul waiteth for the Lord: he is our help and our shield" (33:20). "Thou art my hiding place and my shield: I hope in thy word" (119:114). Proverbs 30:5 says, "Every word of God is pure: he is a shield unto them that put their trust in him."

Although Job did not refer to God as his shield, it is apparent that Job knew this truth experientially, for in his intense suffering he was able to say, "Though he slay me, yet will I trust in him" (Job 13:15). Job also said of God: "He knoweth the way that I take: when he hath tried me, I shall come forth as gold" (23:10).

We must remember that the shield of faith is not something which the believer carries with him. It would be futile for the believer to carry a shield hoping to detect from which direction Satan would throw one of his darts. Satan attacks when we least expect him to, and we would never be able to effectively withstand his attacks if it depended on our intelligence or ability.

The only kind of shield of faith that is effective for us is one which protects us from all sides at the same time. This is exactly what Christ is to the believer. As we have seen throughout the Book of Ephesians, we are "in" Christ. Colossians 3:3 tells believers: "Your life is hid with Christ in God."

The believer is not viewed as hiding behind Christ or just being on the side of Christ, but "in Christ" (Eph. 1:1). Although Old Testament believers were not "in Christ" in the sense that New Testament believers are, the psalmist recognized that the Lord surrounded him: "Thou hast beset me behind and before, and laid thine hand upon me" (139:5).

Notice from Ephesians 6:16 that the believer is expected, by the shield of faith, to quench *all* of Satan's darts: "Taking the shield of faith, wherewith ye shall be able to quench all the fiery darts of the wicked [one]." Observe that it is not just "the fiery darts" but "all the fiery darts." We do this as we exercise our faith in Jesus Christ. God never provides just partial protection for His own; when we trust Him to do what He has said He will do, we have complete protection.

Note that this is a shield of faith. As we appropriate by faith what God has promised, we are "taking the shield of faith." For instance, Romans 6:14 tells us: "For sin shall not have dominion over you: for ye are not under the law, but under grace." As we place our faith, or trust, in this and other truths revealed in Romans 6, we will experience victory over sin in our daily life. Faith itself is a gift from God and comes by the Word of God, for we are told in Romans 10:17: "So then faith cometh by hearing, and hearing by the word of God." As we study the Scriptures we will grow in faith because we will know what God has done and said.

By means of the shield of faith we are to "quench all the fiery darts of the wicked" (Eph. 6:16). Charles B. Williams translates this verse: "Take on the shield which faith provides, for with it you will be able to put out all the fire-tipped arrows shot by the evil one." Let us consider some of the fire-tipped arrows that need to be put out. Satan's arrows, or darts, are his means of attempting to defeat us. He works through various aspects of our lives in attempting to do this.

Satan can attack us by encouraging us to be proud. Proverbs 16:18 warns: "Pride goeth before destruction, and an haughty spirit before a fall." Satan can also attack through the desires of the body. For instance, sexual desire is of God, but Satan may encourage the Christian to satisfy this desire in an illegitimate manner.

When we are tempted to do wrong, we must remember that such a temptation does not originate with the Lord. The Bible says, "Let no man say when he is tempted, I am tempted of God: for God cannot be tempted with evil, neither tempteth he any man: but every man is tempted, when he is drawn away of his own lust, and enticed. Then when lust hath conceived, it bringeth forth sin: and sin, when it is finished, bringeth forth death" (James 1:15).

If we are relying on Christ, Satan's fire-tipped arrows will be put out before they can do their damage. But if we do not rely on Christ to be our strength when temptations come, we will be vulnerable to Satan's attacks and will experience serious frustration in the Christian life.

One of Satan's methods is to attack the believer's thought life. Satan encourages doubts and anxiety which make the believer less effective for the Lord. Realizing that the mind is a spiritual battleground, Paul said, "We are destroying speculations and every lofty thing raised up against the knowledge of God, and we are taking every thought captive to the obedience of Christ" (II Cor. 10:5, NASB). In times of severe stress, Satan especially likes to implant doubt in the Christian's mind concerning God's faithfulness, or concerning the authority or reliability of His promises.

Satan also attacks the believer when he sins and suggests to him that God does not really forgive his sin, or at least that God is holding against him a sin he has committed in the past. The promises of the Word of God are extremely important at such a time. God says, "I have blotted out, as a thick cloud, thy transgressions, and, as a cloud, thy sins: return unto me; for I have redeemed thee" (Isa. 44:22). Isaiah 38:17 records Hezekiah's statements to God: "Behold, for peace I had great bitterness: but thou hast in love to my soul delivered it from the pit of corruption: for thou hast cast all my sins behind thy back." The New Testament states concerning those who are in right relationship with Him: "Their sins and iniquities will I remember no more" (Heb. 10:17).

The basis for such forgiveness is what Christ accomplished when He died on the cross for us. He fully satisfied the Heavenly Father's righteous demands for our sins. Therefore, we are delivered from condemnation by receiving Christ as Saviour. Knowing these truths, we should be faithful in going to the Scriptures to read them again when Satan attacks in this area.

When we go through trying experiences, such as losing our possessions or losing a loved one through death, we need to remember that the Lord has not forsaken us. Although Satan will encourage us to think that God has forgotten us, Hebrews 13:5 assures: "I will never leave thee, nor forsake thee." The Apostle Paul was able to be victorious in adverse circumstances because he had learned to trust Christ regardless of the circumstances. Thus, Paul was able to say, "Not that I speak from want; for I have learned to be content in whatever circumstances I am. I know how to get along with humble means, and I also know how to live in prosperity; in any and every circumstance I have learned the secret of being filled and going hungry, both of having abundance and suffering need. I can do all things through Him who strengthens me" (Phil. 4:11-13, NASB).

Strange things happen to us in God's perfect plan to shape us for eternity. When we become preoccupied in seeking to know why these things are so, Satan is given an opportunity to shoot his arrows of discouragement and doubt at us. Even though we do not understand all that is being allowed in our lives, rather than asking "Why?" we should take the shield of faith by trusting Christ and His Word completely.

When adversity comes into our lives, we need to remember Romans 8:28: "We know that all things work together for good to them that love God, to them who are the called according to his purpose." As believers we can know this truth with certainty even though we cannot understand what God is specifically trying to accomplish in our lives. When we are certain—because of our faith in God—that things are working together for our ultimate good and His glory, we will have a different attitude about difficult circumstances. As verse 31,32 says, "What shall we then say to these things? If God be for us, who can be against us? He that spared not his own Son, but delivered him up for us all, how shall he not with him also freely give us all things?" So when testing comes we need to read such passages as this to remind ourselves that God has a purpose for what He is doing and that He has not made a mistake in our lives.

Concerning suffering, James said, "Take, my brethren, the prophets, who have spoken in the name of the Lord, for an example of suffering affliction, and of patience" (5:10). Paul said, "For I reckon that the sufferings of this present time are not worthy to be compared with the glory which shall be revealed in us" (Rom. 8:18). Although God allows adversity to come in order that we might become more spiritually mature, He does not allow more than we are able to endure. First Corinthians 10:13 says, "There hath no temptation taken you but such as is common to man: but God is faithful, who will not suffer you to be tempted above that ye are able; but will with the temptation also make a way to escape, that ye may be able to bear it." Our trials may seem more than we are able to bear, especially if we do not trust God completely in our suffering, but note especially that He also provides necessary grace so we can escape and bear them. If we are living by faith we will be able to say with Job, "When he hath tried me, I shall come forth as gold" (23:10).

In considering the difficult circumstances that come into our lives, we need to remember that the Lord never tests us for the purpose of causing us to fail. Referring to our incorruptible inheritance waiting in heaven for us, Peter said, "Wherein ye greatly rejoice, though now for a season, if need be, ye are in heaviness through manifold temptations: that the trial of your faith, being much more precious than of gold that perisheth, though it be tried with fire, might be found unto praise and honour and glory at the appearing of Jesus Christ" (I Pet. 1:6,7). The Lord's purpose in discipline is not to cause us to fail but to make us more spiritually mature so we can share in His holiness. The Bible says, "Now no chastening for the present seemeth to be joyous, but grievous: nevertheless afterward it yieldeth the peaceable fruit of righteousness unto them which are exercised thereby" (Heb. 12:11).

There are many other darts that Satan shoots at us; they may be in the form of encouraging us to lose our temper or to harbor resentment. We especially need to be careful when we are criticized because this often gives Satan an opportunity to fire one of his darts at us. The words of Jude are especially fitting for us to remember in this regard: "But ye, beloved, building up yourselves on your most holy faith, praying in the Holy Ghost, keep yourselves in the love of God, looking for the mercy of our Lord Jesus Christ unto eternal life" (vv. 20,21). Colossians 2:6,7 tells us: "As ye have therefore received Christ Jesus the Lord, so walk ye in him: rooted and built up in him, and stablished in the faith, as ye have been taught, abounding therein with thanksgiving."

We take the shield of faith, then, by trusting Christ and His Word completely, which in turn protects us from Satan's fire-tipped arrows.

Helmet of Salvation

The fifth part of armor for the believer is mentioned in Ephesians 6:17: "And take the helmet of salvation." The helmet was for protecting the head, which is the center of the intellectual life of the body. A head wound is a serious matter because the body does not function properly if the head is not functioning properly. The "helmet of salvation" refers to Jesus Christ and reveals that He is the protection for this part of the body.

The psalmist said, "The Lord is my light and my salvation" (27:1). To take the helmet of salvation is to recognize Jesus Christ as the very life of our salvation. Having received Christ, we have eternal life, for the Bible says: "And this is the record, that God hath given to us eternal life, and this life is in his Son. He that hath the Son hath life; and he that hath not the Son of God hath not life" (I John 5:11,12). We will have a great advantage over Satan if we realize that salvation is not just something that the Lord gives, but it is Christ Himself who is given to us.

One of Satan's key attacks in the area of salvation is to cause the believer to doubt his salvation. However, as we have seen, I John 5:11,12 assures an individual that if he has Jesus

Christ, he has eternal life. Satan also causes some to think they can lose eternal life, but Christ said, "I give unto them eternal life; and they shall never perish, neither shall any man pluck them out of my hand. My Father, which gave them me, is greater than all; and no man is able to pluck them out of my Father's hand" (John 10:28,29).

Because the head is the center of our thought processes, Satan will distort our thinking from what God wants it to be if he effectively gets to our minds. For instance, if Satan can cause us to doubt our salvation, he has struck at the basis of all our spiritual functions of life. If, however, we know we have salvation in Christ and are trusting completely in the efficacy of God's saving grace, we have the proper basis necessary for spiritual maturity. As we trust in Christ regarding our salvation, He is the helmet of salvation to us and Satan's attacks are nullified. All the processes of spiritual maturity and an effective life for the Lord depend on the knowledge of our salvation in Christ.

The Bible teaches that the person who places faith in Christ is secure in Him. Concerning Christ, it says, "Wherefore he is able also to save them to the uttermost that come unto God by him, seeing he ever liveth to make intercession for them" (Heb. 7:25). Of believers, I Peter 1:5 says, "Who are kept by the power of God through faith unto salvation ready to be revealed in the last time." Of Christ, I John 2:2 says, "And he is the propitiation [satisfaction] for our sins: and not for our's only, but also for the sins of the whole world." Since Christ has paid the penalty for sin, "as many as received him, to them gave he power to become the sons of God, even to them that believe on his name" (John 1:12). When the believer commits a sin, he does not lose his salvation; rather, he loses fellowship with God. However, this fellowship is restored when he confesses his sin. The Bible says, "If we walk in the light, as he is in the light, we have fellowship one with another, and the blood of Jesus Christ his Son cleanseth us from all sin. If we confess our sins, he is faithful and just to forgive us our sins, and to cleanse us from all unrighteousness" (I John 1:7,9).

Even a true concept of the vital doctrines of the Scriptures depends on an accurate comprehension of salvation being based on the finished work of Christ. To realize from the Scriptures that our salvation is complete in Christ and Him alone, requires that one also believes in the deity of Christ, His virgin birth, His substitutionary death, and His burial and resurrection. If we deny any of these related truths, we deny the efficacy, or effectiveness, of Christ's work on the cross. For instance, if Christ was not born of a virgin, then He would also have had a sin nature and the benefits of His death could not be applied to others. So to believe in salvation "by grace . . . through faith" (Eph. 2:8) presupposes correct beliefs concerning other doctrines. Those who do not believe the Scriptures concerning these other doctrines will teach salvation by works rather than grace because they do not believe that Christ has paid the full penalty for sin.

Satan concentrates many of his attacks at the believer's hope of salvation because if he can succeed in getting us to doubt our salvation he has laid the basis to lead us into error. Thus we see how vital the helmet of salvation is to every believer. Our trust must be in Christ not only for salvation but also for His ability to carry our salvation through to the end.

Sword of the Spirit

The sixth and final part of the armor to be taken by the believer is "the sword of the Spirit, which is the word of God" (Eph. 6:17). The sword of the Spirit is not an instrument to be placed in the believer's hand; it, too, refers to the protection given by the Lord Jesus Christ, even as the other pieces of the armor refer to an aspect of Christ's protection. Notice what the sword of the Spirit is—"the word of God." The Gospel of John refers to Jesus Christ as the "Word," especially in 1:1-14. This Gospel begins: "In the beginning was the Word, and the Word was with God, and the Word was God" (v. 1). This passage concludes: "And the Word was made flesh, and dwelt among us, (and we beheld his glory, the glory as of the only begotten of the Father,) full of grace and truth" (v. 14). These verses reveal that the "Word" refers specifically to the Lord Jesus Christ who left heaven's glory to take upon Himself the form of a man and die on the cross for the sins of the world.

The Bible is also referred to as God's "Word" (note several verses in Psalm 119). As has been indicated previously, the difference is that Jesus Christ is the Living Word and the Bible is the written Word. The two are brought together in Hebrews 1:1,2: "God, who at sundry times and in divers manners spake in time past unto the fathers by the prophets, hath in these last days spoken unto us by his Son, whom he hath appointed heir of all things, by whom also he made the worlds." God gave the written Word through the prophets, and He gave the Living Word when He gave His only Son to come to earth.

Jesus told of the necessity of assimilating the Living and written Word, and His comments are recorded in the Gospel of John. Jesus said, "I am the living bread which came down from heaven: if any man eat of this bread, he shall live for ever: and the bread that I will give is my flesh, which I will give for the life of the world" (6:51). The Jews could not understand how Jesus could give them His flesh to eat. Jesus added: "Whoso eateth my flesh, and drinketh my blood, hath eternal life; and I will raise him up at the last day. For my flesh is meat indeed, and my blood is drink indeed. He that eateth my flesh, and drinketh my blood, dwelleth in me, and I in him. As the living Father hath sent me, and I live by the Father: so he that eateth me, even he shall live by me" (vv. 53-57).

Many turned back from following Jesus because of these words which they could not understand, but Jesus gave the clue to their meaning in verse 63: "It is the spirit that quickeneth [makes alive]; the flesh profiteth nothing: the words that I speak unto you, they are spirit, and they are life." Jesus did not intend for His flesh to be literally eaten; He was emphasizing the need for His message to be completely assimilated and obeyed. It was the same as if He would have told His followers that they needed to feed upon Him and His Word.

The Word is referred to as "milk" (I Pet. 2:2) and "meat" (Heb. 5:14). Thus, the Word is spiritual food for the believer. Jeremiah said, "Thy words were found, and I did eat them; and thy word was unto me the joy and rejoicing of mine heart: for I am called by thy name, O Lord God of hosts" (15:16). By this statement, Jeremiah was saying that he fed upon the message contained in the Word of God. The psalmist said, "How sweet are thy words unto my taste! yea, sweeter than honey to my mouth!" (119:103).

God's written Word came to us by inspiration: "All scripture is given by inspiration of God" (II Tim. 3:16). The Living Word came to us by incarnation: "The Word was made flesh, and dwelt among us" (John 1:14). The written Word (Bible) and Living Word (Christ) are inseparable. The written Word is the message of the Living Word. Those who love the Living Word also love the written Word for it tells about Him. To be careless about our relationship with the written Word is also to be careless about our relationship with the Living Word.

It is the ministry of the Holy Spirit to reveal Christ to the believer (John 16:15), and He does this by revealing to the believer the truths of the written Word. This is why the Bible is referred to as the "sword of the Spirit"; it is the method by which the Spirit works in our lives, making Christ real to us.

Hebrews 4:12 says, "For the word of God is quick [living], and powerful, and sharper than any twoedged sword, piercing even to the dividing asunder of soul and spirit, and of the joints and marrow, and is a discerner of the thoughts and intents of the heart." The power of His spoken word is seen in Genesis 1, for God spoke and the result was creation.

As part of the believer's armor (Eph. 6:17), the Word of God is to be used primarily as a defense against Satan's attacks. Christ Himself gave us an example of how to meet the attacks of Satan by the written Word (Matt. 4:1-11).

The degree to which we will be able to use the sword of the Spirit depends on the degree to which we allow it to penetrate our hearts; that is, to become real and living within us. This involves more than just memorizing the Scriptures; it requires that we respond to the Scriptures by putting the message of the Word of God into action in our lives. It is not enough to know the Scriptures, we must act on the basis of what they say. Even Satan knows what the Scriptures say, but he rejects the message, and even comes as an angel of light quoting it to deceive others. Just as Satan did with Eve, he can raise questions about something God has said and in that way plant doubts in a person's mind. There is no substitute for our knowing what the Scriptures teach and for doing what it requires. As we have seen concerning the believer's armor, it is particularly important that we know what the Scriptures say about our relationship to God.

Not only is the sword of the Spirit, the Bible, to be used defensively against the attacks of Satan, but we are also to use it offensively in seeking to win others to Christ. Jesus commanded: "Go ye into all the world, and preach the gospel to every creature" (Mark 16:15). We should always use the Scriptures when helping someone see his need of Christ. The Bible is the only authoritative Word of God so it is the basis we must use in telling others of their sin and their need to receive Christ as Saviour. Because the Bible is the only authoritative revelation from God, Paul urged Timothy: "Preach the word; be instant in season, out of season; reprove, rebuke, exhort with all longsuffering and doctrine" (II Tim. 4:2).

To be able to use the sword of the Spirit effectively either defensively or offensively calls for the greatest degree of spiritual devotion to Christ. Mere repetition of words does not make an efficient sword. But when the sword of the Spirit is spoken from a heart that is filled with the Spirit, there will be eternal benefits.

The sword must be ready at a moment's notice because Satan attacks without warning. He does not wait until we have our Bibles open and are reading God's Word before he attacks. He often waits for the opposite—when our minds are farthest from the Word. However, even though we may not have the Bible available to read at the moment it can be available if we have memorized portions of it. In times of need, the Spirit will bring to our attention the truths of God's Word if we have spent time thinking deeply on them in the past. It is one of the Holy Spirit's ministries to bring things to our memory: "But the Comforter, which is the Holy Ghost, whom the Father will send in my name, he shall teach you all things, and bring all things to your remembrance whatsoever I have said unto you" (John 14:26). In this way, the Word becomes a sword of the Spirit even though we may not have the Bible available to read. So it is important that we hide the Word in our hearts, even as David did (Ps. 119:11).

It is well to remember that, in witnessing, our responsibility is to set forth the Word; we do not need to defend it. On commenting about the lack of need to defend the Word, Spurgeon pointed out that one does not need to defend the Word any more than he needs to defend a lion; let the lion out of his cage and he will defend himself.

The Results Expected

If we put on "the whole armour of God" (Eph. 6:11), what results can we expect? In considering this, we should remember that the armor is available to all who know Christ and who will appropriate it by faith. No believer has an excuse for any vulnerable spot because the armor is available for full protection.

The results that can be expected when the entire armor is appropriated by faith center in the three occurrences of the word "able" in this passage (vv. 11,13,16). Verse 11 says, "Put on the whole armour of God, that ye may be able to stand against the wiles of the devil." From this verse we see that the appropriation of the entire armor enables us to stand against the Devil's craftiness. Even the weakest believer can overcome Satan by exercising faith in Christ for each aspect of his life. God desires that each believer have a victorious Christian life. With Paul, we can say, "Thanks be unto God, which always causeth us to triumph in Christ" (II Cor. 2:14). We can also echo his words: "Thanks be to God, which giveth us the victory through our Lord Jesus Christ" (I Cor. 15:57). And we can apply Paul's conclusion: "Therefore, my beloved brethren, be ye stedfast, unmoveable, always abounding in the work of the Lord, forasmuch as ye know that your labour is not in vain in the Lord" (v. 58).

So let us expect victory, not defeat. By faith we can conquer! Too many have been defeated simply because they have gone into the spiritual conflict anticipating failure. Let us not forget that we are "able."

The second occurrence of the word "able" is in Ephesians 6:13: "Wherefore take unto you the whole armour of God, that ye may be able to withstand in the evil day, and having done all, to stand." Another result of appropriating the spiritual armor by faith is that we will be able to stand victorious in the evil day. The word translated "withstand" can also be translated "resist," as it is in James 4:7: "Submit yourselves therefore to God. Resist the devil, and he will flee from you." This word is translated "resist" in I Peter 5:9 also: "Whom [Satan] resist stedfast in the faith, knowing that the same afflictions are accomplished in your brethren that are in the world." The armor enables the believer to effectively resist Satan and thus to stand victorious in the "evil day." The "evil day" probably refers to the time of severe temptations and trials.

The only way that we can successfully encounter and defeat Satan is when we are, by faith, entrenched in Christ. This is why James 4:7 first mentions that we are to submit ourselves to God before it mentions that we are to resist the Devil. When we submit to Christ and depend on Him as our fortress, He Himself will be our wall of defense.

The statement in I Peter 5:9 saying that we are to "resist stedfast in the faith" reminds us that we are to stand fast in faith's victorious position. It is evident that the spiritual conflict is a fight of faith. At the end of his life, Paul charged Timothy: "Fight the good fight of faith" (I Tim. 6:12). Of himself, Paul could say: "For I am now ready to be offered, and the time of my departure is at hand. I have fought a good fight [of faith], I have finished my course, I have kept the faith: henceforth there is laid up for me a crown of righteousness, which the Lord, the righteous judge, shall give me at that day: and not to me only, but unto all them also that love his appearing" (II Tim. 4:6-7).

Let us trust the Lord for every detail of our life. If we fail, let us confess our sin to Him and remember that He has promised to forgive when we confess it (I John 1:9). Let us "walk in the light, as he is in the light" (I John 1:7), and we will experience victory over Satan. As we study the Word of God we should let the light of His Word expose any sin and immediately confess it.

The third occurrence of the word "able" concerning the spiritual armor is found in Ephesians 6:16: "Above all, taking the shield of faith, wherewith ye shall be able to quench all the fiery darts of the wicked [one]. Thus we see another result that can be expected when we appropriate the armor by faith—we will be enabled to put out *all* the fire-tipped arrows of the Devil. This is possible by trusting in Jesus Christ who is the shield of faith for the believer. We have carefully examined the verses previously which reveal that Christ is our shield and life and that He lives in and through us (Gal. 2:20; Col. 3:3,4).

Christ is the shield that faith apprehends, and He stands between the believer and Satan so we need never fear. The Lord is with us at all times even as David realized (Ps. 23). As we put our trust in Him He will protect us on every side.

The truth we have seen from the six pieces of armor is that each one presents a different aspect of the way Jesus Christ is the protection for His own. Our responsibility is to place our confidence in Him for each step we take.

Chapter 6

Resources for Victory

(Eph. 6:18-20)

In the Book of Ephesians, prayer reaches the highest pinnacle of any place in the Bible. Two of Paul's prayers are recorded in this Book. The first prayer (1:15-21) was for the believers to have the spirit of wisdom and revelation in the knowledge of Christ. The second prayer (3:14-21) was for believers to have an experiential knowledge of Christ's indwelling work within believers.

In connection with the spiritual armor of believers, another reference is made to prayer: "Praying always with all prayer and supplication in the Spirit, and watching thereunto with all perseverance and supplication for all saints" (6:18). Here we see that in addition to taking on the entire armor of God, believers are to be constantly praying. Prayer is not regarded as part of the armor, but the believer who has on the armor is to persevere in prayer. Romans 13:14 tells us to "Put . . . on the Lord Jesus Christ" and this is done by prayer, for Christ is made real to us through prayer.

In order for believers to stand victoriously in the conflict—even with the complete armor—there must be constant, earnest prayer. It is through prayer of faith that the believer's armor is first put on, and then becomes effective. Since prayer is associated here with warfare, the indication is that prayer itself is part of the battle. Daniel experienced the battle of prayer. He had been praying without answer, and then he said: "Behold, an hand touched me, which set me upon my knees and upon the palms of my hands. And he said unto me, O Daniel, a man greatly beloved, understand the words that I speak unto thee, and stand upright: for unto thee am I now sent. And when he had spoken this word unto

63

me, I stood trembling. Then said he unto me, Fear not, Daniel: for from the first day that thou didst set thine heart to understand, and to chasten thyself before thy God, thy words were heard, and I am come for thy words. But the prince of the kingdom of Persia withstood me one and twenty days: but, lo, Michael, one of the chief princes, came to help me; and I remained there with the kings of Persia" (10:10-13). This gives us an insight into the way principalities and powers seek to hinder answers to prayer.

Our Saviour also knew of the battle of prayer for He agonized in prayer. While He was in the Garden of Gethsemane, He thought about His coming death on the cross "and being in an agony he prayed more earnestly: and his sweat was as it were great drops of blood falling down to the ground" (Luke 22:44). The word translated "agony" refers to a conflict, fight or contest. Here it denotes severe emotional strain and anguish. Jesus was having an intense struggle in prayer because of the cross that loomed before Him.

Prayer is a conflict in itself, and it is vital in the spiritual warfare in which every believer is involved. Notice from Ephesians 6:18 that praying and watching should be done "with all perseverance." This doesn't mean that we defeat Satan by working and striving in prayer, for we have already seen that Satan is a defeated foe because of Christ's work on the cross. However, our agonizing in prayer has to do with our taking our position in Christ as the victorious one. We are to "fight the good fight of faith" (I Tim. 6:12) by means of prayer.

Someone has said, "Prayer is not trying to persuade God to join us in our service for Him. It is joining Him in His service. Prayer is a true Christian laying hold by faith on property which Satan controls but which rightly belongs to God, and holding on until Satan lets go."

Praying in the Spirit

Ephesians 6:17 tells of the "sword of the Spirit"; verse 18 tells of praying "in the Spirit." Just as human weapons are of no value in the spiritual warfare (II Cor. 10:4), prayer that is not in the Spirit is also of no value. A prayer that is lovely to listen to may not necessarily be "in the Spirit." Some believers may not know how to express themselves adequately in prayer before others, but they may be praying effectively in the Spirit.

Prayer is effectual when it has its origin with God. God sees the whole battlefield and knows the Devil's plans. God decides the place and part of every soldier in the conflict, and He directs the movements of the entire spiritual army. Since God sets forth definite objectives to be carried out in His eternal purpose, He must also implant in us our prayers for spiritual victory. God communicates to us through the Holy Spirit the prayers we are to pray. The Holy Spirit lays the proper burden on us and He motivates and gives us the throughts to pray. Romans 8:26 says, "Likewise the Spirit also helpeth our infirmities: for we know not what we should pray for as we ought: but the Spirit itself maketh intercession for us with groanings which cannot be uttered."

So it is God who gives the deep sense of urgency for prayer and also gives assurance of victory. We do not know where Satan has placed his snares and pitfalls, but if we are alert to the Holy Spirit He will stimulate prayer within us so we will be forewarned and fully ready with the provided armor. We should be sensitive to the Holy Spirit's work in our lives as He prompts us to prayer and gives assurance that our prayers will be answered. Even though we do not know what to pray for, the Holy Spirit will prompt us and will pray through us. The Father, through the Spirit, motivates us to pray for what we should (Rom. 8:26,27). Then we, in the Spirit, present our petitions back to the Father in the name of Christ. Someone has said, "Prayer in the Spirit must be Spirit-inspired, Spirit-inwrought, Spirit-taught, Spirit-directed and Spirit-energized." Even in prayer, we can expect God to work in us to give us the desire to pray and then to energize us as we pray (Phil. 2:13).

Praying Constantly

The words "praying always" (Eph. 6:18) suggest alertness as well as praying at all times under all conditions. This is unbroken communion with the Lord, not just set times of coming to Him in prayer. It is good to have definite times set aside to spend in prayer, but throughout the day we should be talking to the Lord as we go about various tasks.

Praying constantly in the Spirit has two significant implications: (1) It is an admission of our ignorance and impotency in spiritual conflict—we do not know what to do and we do not have the power, of ourselves, to do anything. Such prayer is heeding the words of Proverbs 3:5,6: "Trust in the Lord with all thine heart; and lean not unto thine own understanding. In all thy ways acknowledge him, and he shall direct thy paths." (2) It reveals to the Enemy that we are totally depending on God because we do not have supernatural wisdom and power. By means of prayer, we are "strong in the Lord, and in the power of his might" (Eph. 6:10).

The prayer warrior is a paradox: Toward Christ he shows conscious weakness and seeks strength and wisdom; toward Satan he shows strength in Christ and stands firm in the place of victory.

In ourselves we can do nothing, as is evident from Christ's words: "For without me ye can do nothing" (John 15:5). However, in Christ we can do all things, as Paul stated: "I can do all things through Christ which strengtheneth me" (Phil. 4:13). As we claim our position in Christ through prayer, He will always cause us to triumph (II Cor. 2:14).

Ephesians 6:18 instructs that we are to pray "with all prayer." This refers to every kind of prayer—public, private, long, short, audible, inaudible, asking, thanking. The Bible tells us: "Stop being worried about anything, but always, in prayer and entreaty, and with thanksgiving, keep on making your wants known to God. Then, through your union with Christ Jesus, the peace of God, that surpasses all human thought, will keep guard over your hearts and thoughts" (Phil. 4:6,7, Williams).

Persevering in Prayer

Satan fears the believer who knows how to prevail with God in prayer, for he knows that means the omnipotent power of God is being rallied against him. Because of this, Satan will use any device he can to keep us from praying. Sometimes he uses fatigue for if we wait until the end of the day to spend time in prayer with God we will frequently be too tired to pray. Or Satan will use lethargy and encourage us to delay talking to the Lord about our needs. Satan also uses doubt, discouragement and depression to take away our desire to pray. If these do not work, Satan may use problems at work or in the home to preoccupy our thinking and keep us from prayer. But we are to resist Satan in these attempts and are to be "praying always with all prayer and supplication in the Spirit, and watching thereunto with all perseverance and supplication for all saints" (Eph. 6:18). We are to be alert—"watching thereunto with all perseverance."

The best way the believer has of "watching" or keeping on the alert is through the study of the Scriptures. It is from the Scriptures that we learn to know God's mind, and from them we also learn how Satan may sidetrack us. We must always be on the alert and persevere in our watching.

Notice that we are to pray and watch "with all perseverance." That is, we are not to give up or become discouraged when answers to prayer are delayed. Perhaps you have been praying for something for a long time. Have you ever thought about the fact that God knows exactly when to answer that prayer? Our responsibility is to keep on praying and to trust God completely for an answer according to His will in His own time. If God has really laid something on our hearts that is His will to do, we should not pray and then wonder whether He will do it or not. We should pray and then watch how God is going to answer.

Praying for All Believers

Ephesians 6:18 tells us that we are to be praying and "watching thereunto with all perseverance and supplication for all saints." Prayer for all the saints is necessary because we are all in the spiritual conflict together. All believers are members of the Body of Christ and the Bible says, "Whether one member suffer, all the members suffer with it; or one member be honoured, all the members rejoice with it" (I Cor. 12:26). We need to work together as a team. And remember, individuals who excel in team sports may receive much attention, but much of their success depends on their team working effectively together. Let us pray for each other in the spiritual conflict so we will all stand victorious.

Paul was concerned that the Ephesians not only pray for all saints but that they also pray for him in particular: "And for me, that utterance may be given unto me, that I may open my mouth boldly, to make known the mystery of the gospel, for which I am an ambassador in bonds: that therein I may speak boldly, as I ought to speak" (Eph. 6:19,20).

Satan had succeeded in getting Paul thrown into prison but Satan had not succeeded in putting him out of the spiritual conflict. Paul was still able to bind Satan by prayer and he was still able to pray for other believers. Paul was concerned that they pray for him so that he could speak boldly when opportunity arose.

Do you pray for your pastor? He is in the forefront of the battle because he has been called of God to lead a congregation. As a leader, he becomes a special target of Satan's most vicious attacks. If Satan is able to discredit a leader, he is able to discredit Christianity in the minds of many people. No pastor is above the need of prayer. He needs to be supported by prayer so he will be strengthened to utter the Word of God in boldness. Of course, when things are not going well in a church it is easy for the people to complain about the pastor. Few accept seriously the means of prayer that God has provided for changing their pastors into preachers of power—or giving the prayer warrior a better attitude if that is the problem.

Paul was concerned that he might have the message of God to give when opportunity arose; thus, he wanted believers to pray "that utterance may be given to him." Another translation of this verse is: "And for me that a message may be given me when I open my lips, so that I may boldly make known the open secret of the good news" (Williams). Paul was concerned not only that he have a message from God when opportunity arose to give it, but also that he might be able to "speak boldly."

The need today is for the gospel to be given out boldly, not apologetically. Satan blinds the minds of men to the gospel (II Cor. 4:4), so the gospel must be stated boldly in the power of the Holy Spirit if it is going to have an effect. Some have become utterly confused even as to what the gospel really is. They equate the gospel to a message of social action. Whenever people come into a personal relationship with Jesus Christ the effects will be felt by society around them, but the gospel is not social action itself. The gospel is the good news that Jesus Christ has paid the penalty for sin and that anyone can have forgiveness of sin and eternal life by receiving Him as Saviour. Our need then is to speak the gospel distinctly and boldly so others will know what the Word of God teaches concerning sin and salvation. Let us pray that there will be a scriptural understanding of the gospel, and that it will be preached boldly in its purity as God's grace to fallen man and available to all who believe.

From Ephesians 6:10-20 it is obvious that we who know Christ have the responsibility to take our victorious position in Christ against Satan. By prayer we must bind the power of Satan to loose those who are bound. We have been endued with power and authority in Christ Jesus, and as we claim our position in Him we will be able to stand victorious against Satan.

Conclusion

As Paul concluded his letter to the Ephesians, he said, "But that ye also may know my affairs, and how I do, Tychicus, a beloved brother and faithful minister in the Lord, shall make known to you all things: whom I have sent unto you for the same purpose, that ye might know our affairs, and that he might comfort your hearts" (Eph. 6:21,22). Paul's tenderness toward the Ephesian believers is seen in that he sent Tychicus to comfort them because of their concern over his well-being.

Paul ended his letter with the benediction: "Peace be to the brethren, and love with faith, from God the Father and the Lord Jesus Christ. Grace be with all them that love our Lord Jesus Christ in sincerity. Amen" (vv. 23,24).

Paul began his letter with the words "grace" and "peace" (1:2), and he concluded it with the same words invoking God's blessing on those who have entered into the transforming truths of this short epistle. The peace to which Paul referred is available to all who will enter into the victories, and grace is always available to those who claim it. May those of us who know Christ return often to the Book of Ephesians to be reminded of our position in Him and then may we live accordingly, for this is living abundantly.